BY

Lidewij Edelkoort

EDITED BY PHILIP FIMMANO

FETISHISM IN FASHION

FRAM3

CONTENTS

CONTENTS

The Fetishism in Fashion

BY LIDEWIJ EDELKOORT
PHOTOGRAPHY BY MARIE TAILLEFER
ART DIRECTION BY SERGIO MACHADO

We are all born in bondage with a cord around our baby body. An umbilical cord that is the lifeline of gestation and that bonds us to our mother in the most direct and intimate way, connected as we will never be again after birth. The separation anxiety we feel throughout life begins here. This is where the human quest for other forms of connections and bonds starts; unable to replace it, we will try to re-enact or at least remember the primal bond of life.

We are all fed by our mother's nipple or a bottle's teat, and are therefore aware of the early relationship between suckling and surviving and between suckling and satisfaction. These very intimate erotic moments are recalled throughout life and define future desires for flavour and touch. This tactility and taste are both responsible for a liking of skin-type materials and milk-based products, hence the enormous success of ice-cream which is combining both shape and taste, re-enacting the suckling movements.

Most babies are given a safety blanket that is meant to be a partner and protector, a cuddle to be cherished. Some people will hold on to that first bit of cloth for the remainder of their lives and will be very distressed when loosing the cherished object. Therefore this first encounter with fibre and weave is responsible for many of our future encounters with fabric. We will continue to search for the same softness, a similar colour, an equal weight. Guiding the choices of tomorrow.

All these experiences are imprinted in the subconscious and will determine taste and attraction, designing decisions concerning colour, food, objects and fetishes. Therefore much of our fantasies and aspirations are imbedded in early childhood and are often revisited, becoming a fascination for soup, velvet or shoes, for example. Creating fetishistic patterns in choice and collecting, these initial indicators somehow seem to be unshakeable bonds that need to be acted out and satisfied. Childhood experiences of dominant fathers and sensual mothers might be repressed and rekindled, to become a hair or shoe fetish. Riding horse on a father's back or dancing barefooted on daddy's leather shoes can liberate a catalogue of desires. The folklore of fetishism is endless, with neckties, medals, garter belts, hairbrushes, prosthesis and aprons each narrating their own obsession.

Bonding is able to liberate the self to indulge in the freedom of abundance, creating another unknown self. The quest for bonding has grown in recent decades and is seen as quite a normal urge in people, creating visual evidence of belonging through common things such as tattoos, piercings, leather and chains. Manifold bracelets, wrist beads, textile cords and wish ribbons connect us to a pagan past, now becoming mainstream for men and women of any age, race or social standing. Layered T-shirts and multiple bra straps are seen in all cities and on all beaches. Never before has fashion seen so many bands, strings, laces and belts.

Collecting has become a favourite pastime with more and more people accumulating shoes, bags, boxes and bottles, or natural treasures like shells and even skulls. What these objects have in common is that they are cultural curiosities that can contain and hold; our sex, our soul, our spirit. Objects of devotion that allow us to experience an erotic relationship with our choices. Yet they are also objects of worship that permit us to have a direct relationship with nature and our ancestors and spirits – the shamanic aspect of today's culture. The fetish can be contained or be containing, whether it be a shell or a corset, a skull or a harness, a safety belt or a safety blanket. Each time receiving or restricting, the object has the power to condense desire and to absorb fear, to concentrate dreams and to captivate fantasies.

Instinct and object become one. The fetish is a tool that is able to guide our needs into other territories, such as avoiding a fear of sexual organs by imposing a guardian that will help the transition from reality into fantasy. Transposing the attraction onto an object of worship outside the body liberates sexual partners and loosens up the often troubled male/female relationship. Thus the need for fetish fashions comes to the fore.

The tendency towards paraphilia has nourished the luxury industries at the turn of the century, bringing the sexual arousal of objects into the public domain, where power dressing (as in dominatrix) and porno chic (as in slave behaviour) became household fashion terms. The fetish for shoes, bags and watches was complemented with scarfs, veils and shades, acting like contemporary masks. Seductive lingerie came out of the cupboard to take over style, designing corsets and slip dresses as fashion. Bringing back a fetish for frivolous panties. Ultimately a fashion model was pictured on a poster in a masturbating pose, as if to illustrate the arousal of the objects surrounding her. Erotic fantasy codes have made sexual experiences in consumerism acceptable, with the red carpet like a licking tongue underneath it all.

The soles of shoes are coloured scarlet by Christian Louboutin and Manolo's have become a household fetish, both filled with sexual innuendo. Creation in shoe design is outdoing that of all other historical periods, and shows that shoes are probably the most popular form of fetish today. Small female mules hint at a small well-formed sex, while oversized pumped-up sneakers for men are the promise of a powerful instrument. Size matters in terms of fetishism, and holds the secret of the adulation. High heels elongate the female body, inhibiting her movements to create erotic fantasies. The arched allure of the body and foot are empowering, charging like the ultimate female weapon. Stilettos are seen as phallic and will be used as punishment, trampling or penetrating a slave, whereas a worn and weathered running shoe can become an object to lick and love. Nude ankles and feet in men's sandals are also becoming a mainstream fetish. Elevating the dominatrix above the masses, fashion has decided to put women on a pedestal, at once levitating and forbidding, reminiscent of the way a geisha strides and struggles. Chinese feet in bondage and ballerina slippers are reinvented by the youngest generations of shoe designers, sometimes experimenting with orthopaedic styles and crippling animal hoofs to express new ways of willow walking, both revolting and tantalizing. As an object of devotion, shoes are observed, caressed, penetrated, stolen and collected, normalising the Imelda Marcos phenomenon.

The body itself is trained and tortured to become the sculptural object of devotion. And the corset is the garment to symbolise this thirst for perfection. The corset has been a fetish object since the 19th century when lacing became a favourite erotic pastime. The disciplined body is restrained into the perfect shape of submission, the hourglass silhouette. This action is capable of procuring as much pleasure from feeling contained as it is exciting for the worshipper of the modified body. The use of corsets has not been restricted to women; they have been worn by men and are seen today as an accessory to replace the cumber belt worn with a tuxedo. On the gorgeous body of Madonna, the cone-breasted corset has become an erotic classic, the same conical cups that were seen on Yves Saint Laurent's totemic African dresses. The female waist has further migrated from fetishism to fashion in the hands of Jean Paul Gaultier, Christian Lacroix, Dolce & Gabbana and Boudicca, amongst many others, and is shown in music videos, seen on dance floors and even used in wedding dresses.

The swish of petticoats, the rustling of tulle, the murmuring of taffeta and the rippling of satin can hold the promise of pleasure; sounds of textiles in movement are in themselves arousing. Fabrics can be seen as a fetish, with fur representing pubic hair, velvets for intimate parts, lace for secrecy, satin for adultery and leather and rubber for pain and pleasure. Leather signals power and spells sadism, while rubber signals slavery and whispers masochism. These materials evoke an urge to symbolise animal and human skin. Illustrations of this passion for skin have seen a recent surge of fashion photography using animals to show the animistic bonds consumers have developed with their choices. Pictures of movie stars and models with lions, panthers, birds, snakes and crocodiles have dominated the marketing of luxury goods, suggesting that these objects of desire have a soul and a spirit akin to that of the animal in question; quite a cynical idea since the objects themselves are often created with the skins of these very same animals. A need has grown in consumers to physically bond with the animal kingdom, much like the Eskimos who dress up in disguise to pay respect to the hunted animal. Therefore, the recent revival of fur must be seen as a shamanistic need, able to bring people closer to their animal instincts. The brutalism in fetishist fashions is also expressed through wild and primitive textiles, with rustic and archaic detailing. This extreme interest in animals has brought fashion an intriguing array of animal patterns becoming mainstream high-street fashions. Exhibiting the normalisation of fetishism.

Fashion and fetishism have flirted with each other since the 70's when sexual freedom and greater power for females brought new roles to play into the erotic arena, with the woman pictured as a dominant partner, dressed in uniforms, boots, leather and towering platforms able to crush anything in her path. Much is owed to Yves Saint Laurent who brought women pockets, pants, uniforms, the tuxedo, the leather jacket and boots, liberating females with a feminist and intellectual Left Bank mentality. One would only cross the Seine to go dancing in the famous Club Sept.

The Vietnam War protests triggered a movement that made army and air force garments fashionable, ridiculing the rules of power. Camouflage, overalls and strict military shapes have not left fashion since, and keep coming back, nourished by yet another conflict or war in the world. Fassbinder made the sailor an idol of seduction and in *The Night Porter*, Charlotte Rampling incarnated the strong fetishistic symbolism of military dress.

On the other side of the Channel, Vivienne Westwood and Malcolm McLaren opened their first boutique, *Sex*, in 1974 and got arrested several times on charges of pornography. Yet it was in the 80's that Claude Montana set the tone for a more open discourse about the role of fetishism with super-shouldered power women dressed in leather from head to toe, shown to a soundtrack of galloping horses and crackling whips. At the same time, Thierry Mugler

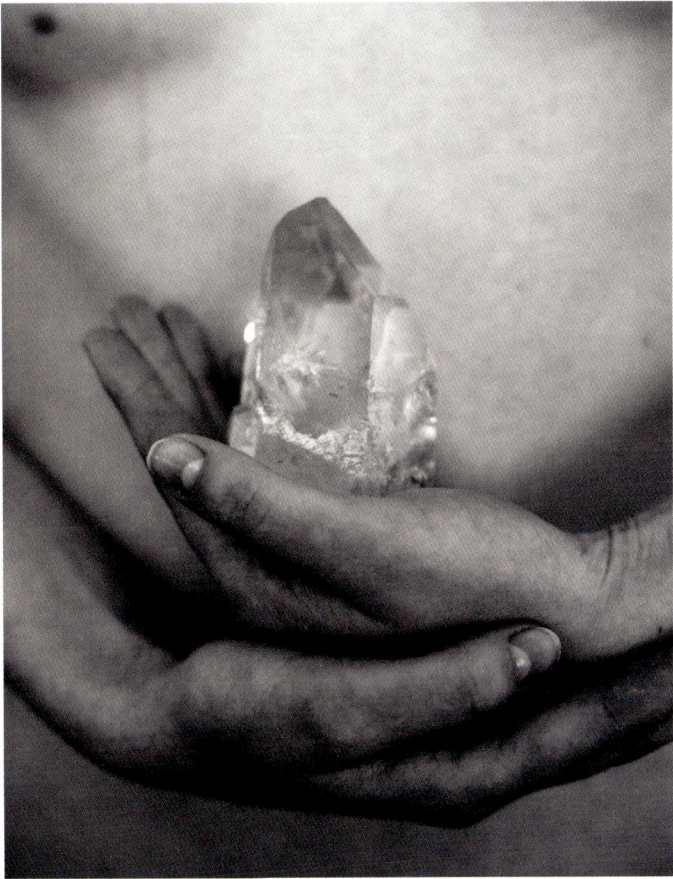
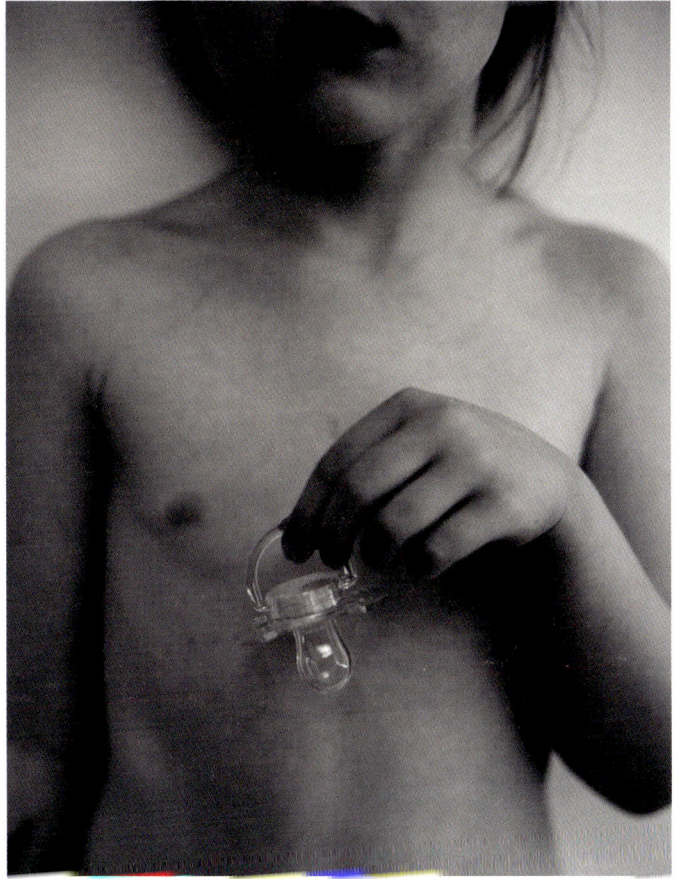

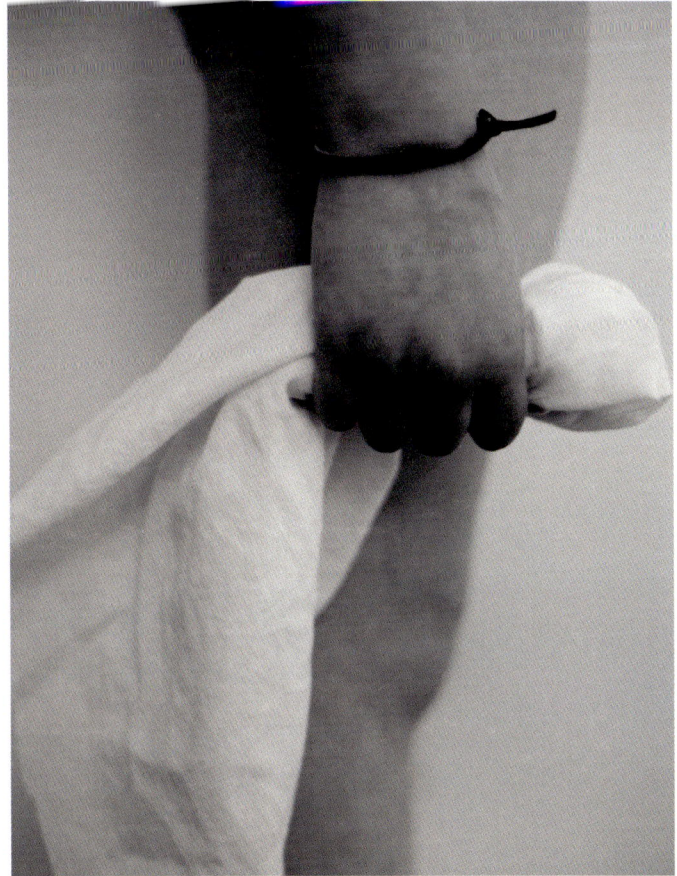

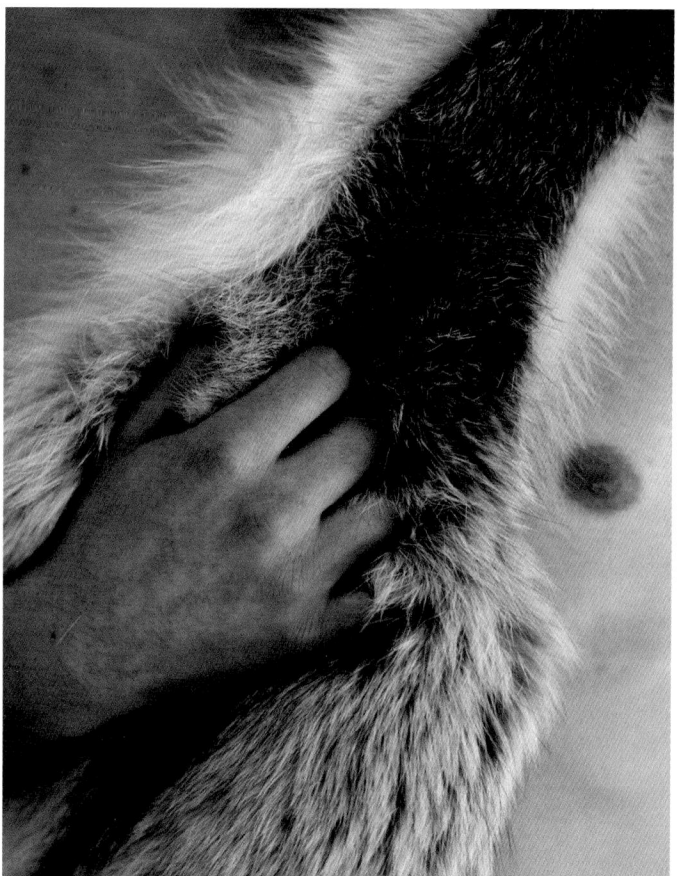

portrayed naughty nurses and perverted nuns playing into the sexual fantasies of men and transvestites. His playful cat women, rendered with humour and malice, would drive the photographers at the end of the catwalk crazy, howling in one voice that expressed their arousal.

At this time, the homosexual world emancipated and went from passive feminine archetypes to assertive masculine ones, using strong ultra-male icons like army and police officers, fire fighters, truck drivers and cowboys, as demonstrated in the 'YMCA' music video by The Village People. With this new behaviour in homosexual circles came the love of leather, metal, studs and belts and a much more fetishist use of bondage, piercing and tattoos. This represented a brutal and raw kind of masculinity, ready to take charge. A celebration of violence. The kerchief was used as a fetish, indicating sexual preferences and chaps would show hidden body parts in broad daylight. Dressed up with aviator sunglasses and a flamboyant moustache. Life seemed to be an endless party and sex was a daily exercise. Until AIDS arrived and arrested the movement, forcing it to go underground and protected. This is when leather and rubber had to become partners in the steaming backrooms of the 90's. Ever since, different fetishist fashions have included softer and more sophisticated notions of idolisation, with supple leathers and furs, pyjamas and slippers, skirts and bowties, and body hair and beards to look like teddy bears

At the beginning of the 70's, the idea of street fashions became important and the first major influence was punk, a powerful movement that rejected consumer society, providing a strong musical moment and a dramatic visual impact to illustrate a "no future" doctrine. It made leathers, studs, chains and safety pins materials that dominated the streets. Hair was coloured and cut into impressive mohawks and in general, allure was intended to scare others. National identities, clans and flags had to be trampled, shredded and worn to pieces. The female punks shopped in sex shops and introduced fishnet stockings, lace T-shirts and stiletto heels to everyday fashions, speaking out loud about fetishism on a bigger scale. At the same time, tattoos and body scarification started to become more common forms of decoration. Somehow, the impact of punk never disappeared, yet it has been modified and mollified in other movements like gothic styles and biker fashions – always in black and desperate – desiring to illustrate a troubled state of mind.

Black is a fetish and a colour with a satanic mentality. It spells out night, danger, death and mourning, and is considered both perverse and powerful. A severe abstraction emanates from this colour that absorbs all other colours and light. It acts like a devouring force that leads to nothingness. Noir has become the mysterious symbol of fetishism in design, manipulating leather, rubber, fragrance, velvet and lace, turning them into frenetic fashions with a strong romantic identity. It is only rivalled by red, the blood of passion, the signal of danger, the pain of menstruation. Therefore, black and red complement each other like night and day.

A love for detail is typical in fetish worship where zips, studs, buckles, belts, fringes, beads, bells and charms introduce a symbolic language of danger and desire. The kinkiness of this attire has attracted both slave and dominatrix alike. General fashion has caught up on these behaviour patterns and dress codes and is lending copious details from the underworld of pain and pleasure to the global world of cult and creation. Resulting in a most amazing display of masked, harnessed, corseted and bondaged designs. Versace, Dolce & Gabbana, Jean Paul Gaultier, Pam Hogg, Azzedine Alaïa and Vivienne Westwood have each continuously delved into the catalogues of sexual attire to discover transformative form and restricting details; fetishizing body parts like the waist, breasts, arms, asses and feet.

The 90's witnessed a growing acceptance of erotic fetishist fashion and actions like piercing and tattoos along with scarification and body modification, as best experienced in the work of the French artist Orlan. Yet the early 90's was also the first moment that anthropological and ecological aspects started to influence design at large, including fashion. Gaia, yoga and meditation entered the lifestyles of many and created an awareness of other, more spiritual values, able to protect people from over-consumption and pop culture. Henceforth, punk's philosophy and spiritual reflection meet and merge in the face of a common enemy. Well-being fashions are minimal and sometimes have a mystical quality with hoods and drapes, fuller sleeves and longer lengths, pointing to an inner awareness. Designers like Donna Karan, Helmut Lang and Zoran lead the way towards spiritual clothes.

Fur inherits a shamanistic quality and carries the spirit of the animal, empowering the human body with animistic principles. When instinct feels at one with a venerated fetish, the soul indulges in the adulation of that object, becoming a subject of devotion. Good luck bracelets become a global fashion and men and women indulge in wooden beads, braided ribbons, trinkets and medallions, sold by the millions.

At the end of last century, craft came back to modify the experience of design and to amplify the thrill of fashion, empowering clothes with embroideries and haberdasheries, celebrating the skills of hands; pointing towards a revival of regionalism. Knitting has returned as a social activity and even as a form of activism, with knitting groups taking over public space, knitting lampposts, road signs, benches and people together. The yarn becomes its fetish and forms a bond amongst people. The comeback of hairy yarns from goats, lamas and even cats, brings more tactile knitwear experiences leading to extreme fetishist behaviour with some men clothed by their knitting dominatrix wives, encased in fluffy knit bodysuits, feeling cosy and kept. With small pouches to contain his balls.

At the turn of the century feminism is turning to femininity to harness the next battles. A young generation born from feminist mothers and grandmothers is choosing pure feminine weapons with which to defend themselves: dresses instead of separates, high heels verses Doc Martins, padded bras over burned ones, legs alternating jeans, and long hair in place of boyish hairdos. Looking like a cross-dressed male, desperate and desirable. They are born and raised with female power and are adamant to exercise this strength with female attributes. This girl power has triggered the normalisation of fetishism in society with ever-higher heels, fuller skirts, deeper cleavage and higher hair, bringing boys to the altar of submission. Yet also searching for the dominant male that doesn't seem to exist anymore, dreaming of Mr Big and of Mr Grey.

Fetishism permeates all creation, theatre and cinema. It becomes a scenario that people aspire to, accepting role play as part of a sexual existence. Therefore, fetishism in fashion is a given, empowering people with tools and textures to express the psychology of power. The 21st century started with a bang when the Twin Towers came crumbling to ground zero. Fear and terrorism replaced the rather happy days of last century and war troubles returned to the public's psyche. The haunting humiliating images from Abu Ghraib uncovered the fetishism of power. Growing unease about our poor mutilated planet has fed the nausea connected with overconsumption, which in turn has triggered a need for recycling and an urge for the reincarnation of matter.

Design has come to the forefront and plays a dominant role, electing primitive materials. Prehistoric bones and organic constructions are inspiring a caveman culture that bring fashion and design to a shamanistic aesthetic, using grasses, beading, furs and skins. 3D printing further inspires a bold organic language that somehow further fuels fetishist form. Computer engineered design brings more biological mimicry. Joris Laarman, Bart Hess and Iris van Herpen are all Dutch designers that create such a universal avant-gardist language. Cyber sex opens yet another door with a myriad of modes encountering virtual flirting and a new slick aesthetic taken from mangas and games. Lara Croft and Annlee become the robotic erotic archetypes that are streamlined by animation technology, rendering things distant and clinical. Safe sex that will further influence fetishes towards other and unknown objects and materials. The future of these characters and their wardrobes will inspire fashion, bringing a need for techno matter that is able to breathe and connect, a transformation of skin into second skin, of

skeleton into dress, of hair into fur, acting as an extension of the human body. Another tactile chapter in the making.

Yet another fetish to become influential in the new millennium is infantilism, the sexual and emotional refusal of grown-ups to grow up. Therefore people regress into baby clothes and toddler toys, in oversized baby cots with giant rattles, in order to feel small, helpless and in need of pampering. Even our food starts to look like baby food with smoothies, soups and purees ready to be spooned. This important trend sees making students love the Teletubbies and adults listen to Chipmunk music. Disney is expanding with fairytale movies made for mature people. A naive and narrative type of fashion is the result, with smocked dresses and bloomers, all-in-ones and bibs, singlets and diapers. A pink and blue craze.

The latest fetish that will conquer our culture is related to the shaman and his capacity to talk with the spirits, using idols to enable people to replace their god by a multitude of metaphysical beings; connected to different talismans, whether it be a stick, a stone or a piece of cloth. Humble everyday objects can attach us to a different place, another time or an alternative state of mind. Our smartphones and tablets could therefore be considered amulets too. These ordinary objects are without monetary value and become the residences of the spirit. They are worn or carried to bring success in loving, hunting, planting, fishing and shopping. The object is often used as a gris-gris to ward off a bad omen. The current movement towards the use of unfinished fur and reptile skins, horn and marble, pearl and its mother, as well as wood and metal in industrial design, all predict fashions and objects that will become animistic and ritualistic, layered with another strength. After all, the word fetish comes from the Portuguese and means artificial (as in manmade), and was used to designate the amulets and deities they saw worshipped by the people of West Africa. Therefore, a more primitive aspect of the current fetish mania is fitting and to be expected. Colouring fashion brown instead of black.

Haughty erotic designs will hereby copulate with humble shamanistic craft to direct style for the future. A perfect hybrid moment where the two brain halves meet and communicate, electing a third movement forward. Erotic and esoteric, these newer creations will blend the natural and the manmade in a co-created universe where sex and spirit somehow merge. Like taking a dominatrix to the Galapagos Islands and coupling her with giant tortoises. Our current times are situated here, forcing a highly creative generation to discover wilder form with organic ornaments and restricting details, yet also containing an elevated spiritual component. The growing social and economic unease is canalised by this growing mental awareness. Using fetishism to endure life and to simply exist.

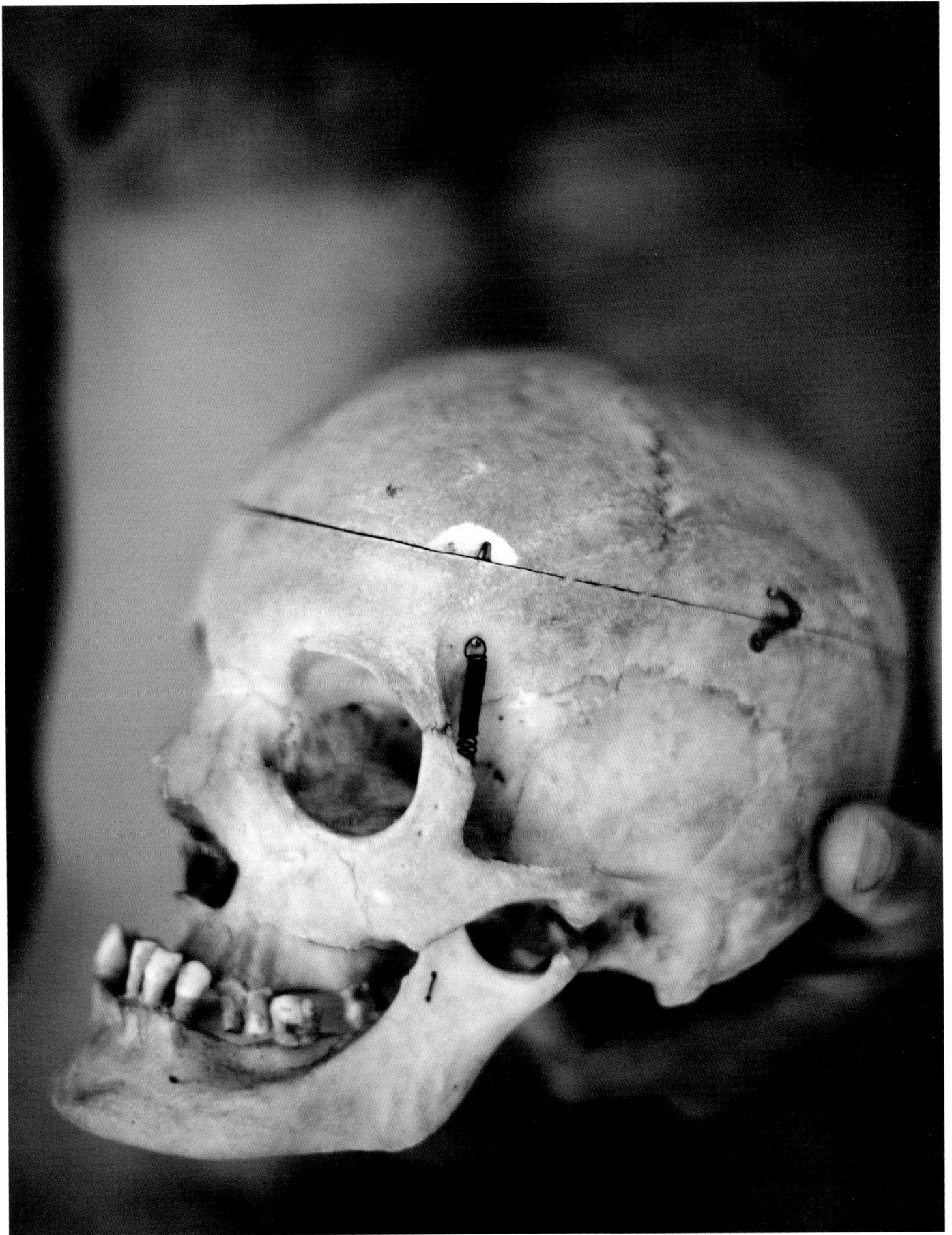

Thirteen Fetishes

BY LIDEWIJ EDELKOORT
PHOTOGRAPHY BY MARIE TAILLEFER
ART DIRECTION BY SERGIO MACHADO

NUDISM

This long-lasting trend that uses the colours of our own skin to imply that we go through life stark naked, is finally coming of age. Since its emergence towards the end of last century, the nude movement hasn't gotten a wrinkle. Fashions and accessories even expose our framework and bone structure, exploring clothing designed from skin and skeletal material, recently inspiring garments that will support, portray and modify nakedness by using prostheses and body adjustments. From the influence of the artist Orlan to the Donut Heads in contemporary Japan, the idea of transforming the face and the body has become a major obsession, with implants and the removal of flesh and bone. Our natural state of being colours textiles bare and gives a raw and undressed dimension to any garment; naturalism in styling is therefore a fetishistic principle, able to transform the way we dress. Materials are epidermic and erotic, exciting the senses with rubberised coatings, organdie veils, whispering satins and fragrant leathers. These materials are configured in corsets, lingerie and bodices that reveal the anatomy of the body and its inner workings. The silhouette has a clinical, dissected style that is deconstructing things even further, penetrating the organs in forever wilder and weirder fashions.

SADO-MASOCHISM

Sadism and masochism have become an important part of culture, enabling us to explore the influence of sex and bondage on fashion. The human perversion of relating pain and pleasure to captivity and control has reached the public arena, and fashion has been a malicious witness to this, expressing a growing fascination with evermore daring designs stolen from hardcore sex shops and steamy backrooms; giving fashionable form to restraining devices and enslaving corsets, merciless bridles and commanding chains, cruel harnesses and unforgiving straitjackets. All to be worn with masks and veils for anonymity. Fashion designers are focussing on disciplined dresses that help initiate the slave to the whims of the master. At this time, the borders between sex shops and luxury brands are hard to define and the range of clothing and accessories inspired by sado-chic is overwhelming. Leather, latex and lace are being used for the construction of corsets and crinolines, with spandex and lycra for bodysuits and hermetic facemasks. Punishment is embedded into beautiful materials and desirable details like spikes, pins and clasps. With brutal belts and erotic laces, the wearer will be tied up in distinct soft forms of sado-masochism. Indeed the term fashion victim will get its final fetishistic interpretation.

INFANTILISM

The latest fetish to be discovered and cultivated by fashion is the young trend of infantilism, where the use of baby clothes, diapers and cuddling textiles expresses a need for being cared for and insinuates a wish to never grow up – immature and overindulged behaviour that mimics the early stages of life. Born and raised in difficult times, a new generation decides not to grow up and remain babies or toddlers all their lives, prolonging the carefree puerile period. Sexual practices include enlarged baby cots and giant rattles to enact babyish behaviour, as well as giant pacifiers to make one feel small, demanding to be nursed, spoiled and spanked, and give the adult a baby experience. This fetishistic need for pampering will have its effect on fashions that will choose soft fabrics and even softer mohair knits, to be used for enlarged babywear in grown-up garments that toy with a colour card of juvenile pastels. The kiddults, as they are called, will dress in all-in-ones and hand-me-down dresses, in smocked and flowered bloomers, neatly pleated diapers and romantic pleated bibs. This new fashion will soon come of age and start to influence many other trends, bringing a fresh and naive aspect to design.

NIPPONISM

Because of its lack of space and island location, Japan has developed a strong bond with the environment, using the earth for pottery, dried grass for basket weaving, the land for tea and rice, and shadows for contemplation; even honouring the spring blossom in an annual festival. In their own special way, the Japanese rule nature and manage the landscape, canalising its rivers and governing ponds, pruning bonsai, restraining flowers and also bondaging their lovers. In fact, they shepherd and master all living things. This need to restrain and contain, to reign in the bridle of destiny, can be seen as a need to tame the inner dragon. The Japanese people have an innate knowledge of how to package and fold geometry into form. Therefore, the flat kimono comes alive when enveloping the female frame, bound together by the unforbidding obi, adorned with ribbons, decorated with gris-gris, and elevated to the extreme on wooden platforms. This amazing allure has forever fascinated fashion and it can possibly be considered the most fetishistic culture in the world, where each rule and move is codified and all aspects are about attachment. Theirs is an aesthetic of arranging the transient and mastering the beauty of the undone. The obsessive side of the Japanese is an interesting hotbed – music to the ears of fashion victims – with sexualised undertones that add a hidden layer to fetishism.

SPIRITUALISM

Humans are deepening their relationship with the mystical and other states of consciousness. Trying to find space and time to reach out to the other, learning how to be more inclusive of the parent, partner, pet, plant or even the planet. A holistic notion of interconnecting and communicating with the world; that weird place of perpetual becoming. A desire for transcendence will be essential to existence. This societal change will be translated into modest fetish fashions using layering and covering, where the veil and the scarf will provide shelter and are at the core of an esoteric inspiration. In order to cloak the body and reveal the soul, clothes are flowing and roomier, with longer lengths, embedded details and hooded coats. Variations of whites with subtle differences are used like an illumination. The religious rigour of black gives character to otherwise minimal clothes in a quest for inner peace. Time and space for concentration allow devotion to detail in an attempt to design harmony, for a new and transformative fashion that is to be revealed. Giving style and substance to ethereal form. People will go through life as pure as modern monks and fashion virgins.

ABSURDISM

The absurdist philosophy teaches us to accept the chaotic disorder of existence, and to become intuitive enough to improvise life as we go along. Some people are currently experiencing a sense of estrangement that forces them to accept the status quo and give in to the rampant madness of the moment. The great disparities between rich and poor will further ignite this trend, seeing the comeback of the political cabaret and burlesque satire. A surreal society where freakish fashions will be supported by strange masks and distorted make-up in order to develop a fictive self, setting the soul free. A sense of disaffection that invites people to explore the bizarre, playing with preposterous proportions, a grotesque style that becomes a humoristic protest against the current state of affairs. Therefore, fashion and design will embrace the bizarre and the deformed with a satanic sense of pleasure, creating monster-like clothes that defy the laws of gravity, going bonkers like a kind of fashion therapy. Fabrics flirt with scale and pattern and juggle with melodrama, playing the buffoon and endorsing the foolishness of fashion. Cross-dressing and clown-dressing will become the norm, with a sense of disguise that has only two functions: to amuse and to seduce.

ROMANTICISM

The term romanticism has been used in reference to artists and philosophers in history, yet it is now used to refer to the poetic and intellectual trends that characterise our future. The worshiping of nature, a wish for wandering and nostalgia for the past will once again motivate society. A place where imagination is celebrated over reason. These new romantics will cherish the freedom of expression and dwell on things like unhappiness. A beautiful feeling of loss. The good old days are idealised and cherished, and hold endless archives for designers. The pain felt when reflecting on the past is essentially a fetishistic romantic moment; feeling homesick for a place, remembering an image, or aching for a landscape. A fascination with the darker side of life is the result, voting for shadow over light, a way of coping by deepening the trauma of existence. Grief is glorified and visualized with suffering slim bodies, porcelain skin, dramatic red hair, theatrical black garments and saccharine detailing; with a fetish for haberdashery, bows, corsets, handkerchiefs and lace. The bittersweet longing for things lost is forcing fashion to choose exquisite and emotional materials. A sentimental journey in time.

LEGENDISM

A saga of fiction and superstition is evolving in fashion today, giving classical icons a dramatic cinematic quality, as if the Gladiator meets Cleopatra. With allegoric aspects and bestial citations, design reinvents itself on the wings of desire. Fascinating fetishistic creations of contemporary clothing acquire a legendary and mythological character. Fables narrate heroic stories about beautiful men and women fighting the fashion police at all costs. Epic moments in culture point towards a revival of a solid society and a growing economy. A positive tale where sweeping trails, embroidered bodices and amazing silks are all figments of our imagination. The Golden Globes and the gilded Oscars will further become places of dreams and drama. The use of armour is victorious, with hammered and embellished surfaces to project a glorious future. Fantasy has no borders and is used to design harnesses and corsets, headdresses and crowns. Shoes are otherworldly creations and seem to carry the wearer like royalty. The use of tarnished metal and aged gold as both a material and as a colour, helps create fashion legends. Icarus and Aphrodite are ready to influence our way of dressing, while this movement also points to the important revival of the decorative arts.

CONSUMERISM

Consumption and fast fashions are consuming our planet and exhausting our resources as well as damaging the environment. Consumerism hunts for and devours the it-bag and the it-dress, turning fashion and style into a rather old-fashioned and degenerated domain; actually, something shameful. This erosion of popular culture is now getting a backlash from its very own young designers, turning against the current situation with humour and dedication. A new generation has developed a hate of throw-away fashions and the over consumption of goods, responding with creative and explosive, very fetishistic clothing. It sometimes seems like the contents of a trash-can have been emptied out onto a garment. They are peddling their clothes and accessories like a social critique, representing the disintegration of the system in a single sculptural outfit – using waste to warn the world. A distaste of fashion that transcends the idea of recycling and collage through the enormous power with which these creations come to life. A wear-and-tear collection of textiles that belong to our consumer culture of packaging, wrapping, taping and wasting. Using mostly photo-printing and collage on polyester and nylon fabrications. Rendered in outlandish brights with eccentric intensity.

REGIONALISM

Tales from historical and folk vernaculars are part of a regional fervour that is inspiring a lifestyle based on the past, yet taken into the future through our newly connected way of living. Abandoning the urban in favour of the rural, contemporary folklore is able to restore a form of sentimental regionalism and romantic localism, which is seen as an antidote to global culture. Society is intrigued and attracted to everything regional and local; unplugged music, territorial dialects, handcrafted design and homemade recipes. While our ancestors' style may have been passed on by an oral tradition, with religious and even mythic elements, home-grown ideas also concern themselves with the ordinary rituals of everyday life. This is a culture of popular beliefs that attaches values to ways of dressing and adorning. Here, the hands are cherished in the celebration of the handmade and the hand-embellished. Fashion reacts to this with almost comical folk dance costumes, with feminine puffed sleeves, fetishistic crinolines, embroidered knitwear, romantic aprons and provincial haberdashery. In a refrain of very bright and optimistic colours. The slow food movement is creating a slow movement in fashion and design, where products are local, resources are regional and retail is just around the corner.

PATRIOTISM

Impressed by YouTube videos and press photography of clashes, rebellion, protests and terrorist attacks, as well as fighting and boxing in streets and stadiums, fashion has turned to patriotism as a new mantra for streetwear and casual design. Hardened by the hardship of being young in troubled times, the world is witnessing a growing need for feelings of belonging and cherishing the land. With chauvinistic flair and arrogant assurance, the youngest cult designers pull out their local flags and regional textiles to establish a heirship to style. They also mix heritage ideas together, such as references to Hell's Angels' leather, Scottish clans, Palestinian scarves, American motorbikes, Punk knitwear, Asian embroideries, Japanese indigos, French sailor stripes, Dutch folklore and rebel denim. Creating a patriotic melting pot of clashing customs and tastes. Styling includes scarves and hoods, rubber-printed sweatshirts and embroidered blousons, patchwork stripes and shredded jeans. These garments will have a hooligan-like character with many aggressive and fetishistic details and accessories. References to the martial arts as well as protective details from football and ice hockey are processed into masks, kneecaps and trainers. This trend illustrates an underground spirit that is able to inspire the masses to update street style with new subcultural codes. A tradition revisited, a patrimony patented.

NOMADISM

Now that our smartphones and tablets have set us free, we are able to work and play everywhere and anytime. As a result, we no longer need a desk or office and are able to completely reinvent our existence. People will again become nomadic and are going back to the beginning of time when our species would roam and wander, living from hunting, fishing and gathering. The fact that business has become entirely universal will make working global and fashion will therefore become nomadic, going on the road for inspirations from itinerant tribes and migrant movements. From desert bedouins to the first pilgrims to the most modern urban nomads. The romantic essence of travel by foot will spur a new vision for outerwear designed for hiking, biking and walking. A casual approach where urban and rural influences are both given place in the creative process, resulting in hybrid clothes for both town and country. Materials are waterproof and welcoming for clothes that cover us to shield against severe weather conditions. These roving fashions are inspired by tents and luggage, with a fetishistic sense of detailing for masks, hoods, straps, laces and velcro to give an explorer's rigour to style.

SHAMANISM

The shaman is born as a sacred envoy between our world and the world of the spirits, and uses trance to reach a form of visionary ecstasy. He can leave his body in search of answers and his anima travels to retrieve ancient wisdom. He works on skills such as healing, divination and hunting for lost souls. Dance and music guide a mystical bond to nature and provide a way for people to share a spiritual experience. The shaman uses his voice to impersonate animals and his drum is a tool for communication with the other dimension. Fetishistic symbols such as sacred shells, animal bones and tell-tale twigs adorn the tambourine and represent the forces of nature. An anthropological study of style is currently exploring other ways of dressing. A divine inspiration ready to transform fashion, translating a spiritual sense of ecology and place. Clothes are covering and cultural, expressing magical functions and animistic belief patterns. Directly inspired by shamanism, cloaks and coats are embroidered and embellished with fringes and feathers. Embroidered belts, hammered bells and carved ornaments are examples that inspire contemporary fetish interests in gris-gris and charms. After all, shamans are trend forecasters and their capacities are close to omnificence, fortune telling decades into the future.

Useless Man: Leigh Bowery
(1961-1994)

BY SYLVIA CHIVARATANOND
PHOTOGRAPHY BY FERGUS GREER

Leigh Bowery, the iconic fashion designer, club promoter, art muse, dancer, performance artist, musician, and human extraordinaire was born in 1961 in Sunshine, Australia, a sleepy suburb outside of Melbourne. From early childhood Bowery felt out of place growing up in a conventional family, with conventional values; little did anyone know that he was to become an unconventional hero to the most unconventional group of individuals at the intersection of art and life. Bowery remains instrumental not only within the dialogue of performance art but also fashion, in all its glories and horrors. Known for being larger than life both physically and metaphorically through his outrageous clothes and antics, Bowery transgressed the boundaries of beauty and gender.

After moving to London in 1980, Bowery soon became entrenched in the underground club scene. Known for dressing provocatively, Bowery would set out every night to a club or to his own performances, either planned or spontaneous, boasting a multitude of body piercings, rivalled perhaps only by the sequins he donned. It was during these early years as an amateur yet meticulous costume designer that he became well known in the gay and transvestite club circles of London and New York. He defied the vernacular of a "camp" or "trash" aesthetic as his garments ranged from a skin-tight full body leather body suit and mask to a tutu as a headpiece with gingham chaps. Physically, Bowery was not your typical beautiful dandy; he was a large man with a fierce attitude who would command the room, often provoking terror in one instant and pathos in the next. Bowery's "look" was as much about self-deprecation as it was about self-hatred; equal parts humour and self-loathing. As the filmmaker Baillie Walsh wrote, "He was really, really horrified by what he looked like. But that was the point, that's why he did it, because he was horrified. He wanted to push it, you know. He wanted to tell you the joke – he didn't want to be the joke."

In 1984, Bowery met the British choreographer Michael Clark, with whom he would later collaborate on numerous costume designs for his ballets, and later became an active member of his dance troupe. The following year he was tapped to be the principle persona at the London club Taboo, soon attracting a regular crowd of admirers including Boy George, Sade, Derek Jarman and John Galliano, among many others. It was also at this time that he met the visual artists Cerith Wyn Evans and Charles Atlas, as well as Nicola Bateman, his soon to be life-long companion and collaborator. Bowery was unique in that he was not simply just a

Session II, Look 7, July 1989

designer of concepts, but would devote a great amount of detail to every "look" or costume he designed for himself and his friends, whether they went to an event or out for a stroll to the corner bakery. Visually, even though he looked like nothing that came before him and often teetered on the horrific, there was something strangely familiar about his fashion fetishes, even when his man-breasts were accentuated in a twenty-inch corset along with a stylized Nazi helmet and heavy make-up. Bowery's relentless desire to take centre stage at every event later developed into a systematic approach to re-writing the body's grammar. He also viewed the many identities he took on as his way of "becoming" the person(s) he had always wanted to be so that he would not have to confront his real self out of costume, which happened almost rarely. Indeed, Bowery was always "on."

Bowery burst onto the scenes of fashion, dance, music and art in London during the 1980s. Embraced by the sub-culture of clubs, his outlandish clothes and make up made him a permanent party fixture on the dance club circuit. More than drag queen but not quite a performance artist. His hand-made spectacular costumes and serial identities were characterized as a reaction against the discord of British daily life under Margaret Thatcher's stringent social and economic policies. In challenging the boundaries of pure artifice during this time in a culture obsessed with authenticity, Bowery mastered the overall use of his body as both subject and material for his art. Increasingly, he used the dance floor, the street, his apartment and the photographer's studio as a proscenium. Between 1988 and 1994, Bowery sat formally in a studio for the London photographer Fergus Greer, documenting countless costumes and personas. Bowery knew that in order for his identities to live on they would have to exist on their own for the public to consume. During this period, his intense practice in taking on the personas he created became more extreme, taking on a more sculptural and abstract form, such as in 1989's *Session II, Looks 7, 8, 9* and *10* and *Session IV, Look 20* from 1991. In these photographs, Bowery obliterates any conception of the body, covering his entire head with a pompom and impregnating himself; his body parts completely engulfed by warped arms and legs.

By 1993 Bowery's confrontational performance style was widely acknowledged as an important contribution to contemporary dance (with Michael Clark) and performance art, including irreverent concerts with his rock band Minty and the troupe Raw Sewage. One of Minty's most well known songs was a track called 'Useless Man.' In one of his most memorable and controversial acts, Bowery gave birth to a full-grown woman on stage. Defecation, urination, blood and vomiting were common features in his performance on stage. During the last four years of life, Bowery was a muse of the pre-eminent British painter Lucian Freud. The intimate paintings of Bowery – the man – captured an enigmatic balance between his abrasive intensity and calm repose in an honest reflection of a human being who has been described as a "beautiful monster."

The Corset

BY VALERIE STEELE
FASHION BY IRIS VAN HERPEN
PHOTOGRAPHY BY BART OOMES

As Foucault reminds us, the body has been subject to various kinds of "disciplinary power." The relations of power "invest it, mark it, train it, torture it, force it... to emit signs."[1] Many feminist scholars have argued that the female body, especially, has been the site of disciplinary regimes, such as dieting and feminine dress, which are designed to make women docile and "feminine." In this context, the corset, in particular, has been interpreted as an instrument of physical oppression and sexual commodification. But the corset has also been praised for its erotic appeal, and the art historian David Kunzle has even argued that so far from being oppressed by their corsets, nineteenth-century tight-lacers were sexually liberated female fetishists who found physical pleasure in the embrace of the corset.[2]

The Votaries of Tight-Lacing

The corset, like the shoe, was one of the first items of clothing to be treated as a fetish, and it remains one of the most important fetish fashions.[3] But it is crucial to distinguish between ordinary *fashionable* corsetry as practiced by most nineteenth-century women and the very different minority practice of *fetishistic* tight-lacing, which sometimes overlaps with sado-masochism and transvestism. Although most Victorian women wore corsets, they were not usually tight-lacers with 16-inch waists anymore than most women today wear fetish shoes with 7-inch heels. The journalist Susan Faludi confuses fashion and fetishism when she writes: "Victorian apparel merchants were the first to mass-market... lingerie, turning corsets into a 'tight-lacing' fetish."[4] But there was never mass-market corset fetishism. Only a handful of corset manufacturers catered to the fetishist market, producing unusually small corsets for women – *and men.*

The corset has aroused more controversy than any other item of clothing. There are two basic reasons: one medical, the other textual – and sexual. It is beyond the scope of this book to analyse the medical literature on corsetry, but a medical doctor, Lynn Kutsche, and I have found that most claims of corset-induced disease are either completely invalid or greatly exaggerated. There is also no evidence for the popular idea that Victorian women had their ribs removed. The use of textual sources has also been extremely naive. Faludi, for example, writes:
In every backlash, the fashion industry has produced punitively restrictive clothing and the fashion press has demanded that women wear them. 'If you want a girl to grow up gentle and womanly in her ways and feelings, lace her tight,' advised one of the many male testimonials to the corset in the late Victorian press.[5]

The notorious advice to "lace her tight" has often been quoted as "proof" that Victorian girls and women were forced to undergo painful, "rib-crushing" tight-lacing as part of a deliberate policy of female oppression. Yet this quotation comes from one of the most suspect sources imaginable: the infamous "corset correspondence" published in *The Englishwoman's Domestic Magazine.*

Between 1867 and 1874, *EDM* printed hundreds of letters on corsetry and tight-lacing, often with a pronounced sado-masochistic tone. There were also related letters on topics such as whipping girls and spurs for lady riders. Many historians have uncritically accepted the bizarre accounts of tight-lacing in *EDM* as being evidence of widespread corset torture during the Victorian era. Susan Faludi, however, apparently did not actually even read the *EDM* correspondence. Instead, her main source for information on corsetry was my book, *Fashion and Eroticism*, from which she selectively drew the quotation from Moralist's letter.[6] I was therefore annoyed, although not particularly surprised, to see how she either misunderstood or wilfully misinterpreted the evidence I presented.

To characterize Moralist's letter as among "the many male testimonials to the corset in the late Victorian press" is extremely misleading, since tight-lacing was almost universally anathematized in the nineteenth century. The *EDM* letters and their successors are highly unusual in defending the practice. Presented out of context, the letter apparently links corsetry with women's oppression. But if the letter is read in conjunction with others of the same genre, Moralist's enthusiasm takes on a very different significance.[7]

Certainly, the *EDM* correspondents had priorities very different from those of the average Victorian woman. Their preoccupations fall into three categories: (1) extreme body modification, which involved wearing tight corsets day and night; (2) a sadomasochistic delight in pain and an emphasis on erotic scenarios involving

dominance and submission; and (3) corsetry as an element in cross-dressing. Fakir Musafar, also known as "the Ol' Corsetier," is probably the most famous corset enthusiast alive today. He says that he learned about tight-lacing in part by reading sources like *EDM*, which "had a pretty fetish-y concept going."[8]

The self-proclaimed "votaries of tight-lacing" described undergoing tight-lacing to extreme tenuity. Other "fetishist" periodicals also claimed that young women were having their waists reduced by as much as 10 inches. Nelly G., age 15, was allegedly reducing her waist from 20 to 16 inches by wearing a tight corset day and night.[9] Even more extreme was "Bertha G., Waist 11 Inches, Age 15," who was sanctimoniously described as "A Child Martyr."[10] If you mention these figures to modern audiences, they gasp with horror. Already conditioned to believe in Scarlett O'Hara's (fictional) 16-inch waist, they seldom question even the most extreme claims. Yet the tight-lacing letters are not necessarily true. When I brought the male tight-lacer, Pearl, to the Costume Institute of the Metropolitan Museum of Art, he was disappointed to find that few of the corsets we saw were as small as his own 19-inch stays.[11]

Corsets were usually advertised as 18 to 30 inches. Larger corsets of 31 to 36 inches were also widely available, and some advertisements mention sizes of 37 inches and above. Of the hundreds of corset advertisements I have examined, less than half a dozen mention corsets of less than 18 inches. One advertisement for "very small-waisted corsets" gives figures of 15 to 26 inches, and may have been targeted at a tight-lacing clientele. The tiny waists mentioned in sources like *EDM* were not at all typical of Victorian women. Yet so notorious is the correspondence that an exhibition on Victorian fashion at the Costume Institute of the Metropolitan Museum of Art captioned a display of corsets with a quotation from the *EDM* letters!

Given the extremes of human behaviour, I cannot say that there was never any such thing as a 16-inch waist. Indeed, I know from contemporary evidence that waists smaller than that can and do exist – as we will see. But the historical evidence shows that in the past, as today, such waists were rare. It is, therefore, time to discard the myth of the 16-inch waist as a touchstone for thinking about the nineteenth-century woman.

In 1994, the magazine *Verbal Abuse* published an interview with Pearl conducted by the dominatrix Mistress Angel Stern, who saw "corsetry as a fetish for number and for measurement." Pearl replied that "the waist-size magic-number is eighteen. Any number below eighteen becomes extremely potent – yes I would say magical."[12] Pearl's idol, Fakir Musafar, a key figure in the world of body modification,[13] has identified "three basic types of people"

who wear corsets today. First, there are what he calls the "corset nonconformists," i.e., people who want to "change the shape of the body... and realize some kind of aesthetic ideal." (This is, presumably, the category in which he would place himself.) Second, there are the "corset identificationists," who associate corsets with "femininity and feminine undergarments." They are not necessarily particularly interested in "sculpting the body" (i.e., tight-lacing), "but by wearing the corset they seemed to have a kind of gender transformation." (He does not say so specifically, but many transvestites fall into this category.) Third are the "corset masochists" who tight-lace "to create erotic discomfort."[14] Considerable overlap exists between these categories, and some people do not fit neatly into any one category. There are also, of course, the followers of fashion – fewer today than in the last century, but not to be discounted.

Discipline and Punish

"One might imagine that in the world of SM roleplay, the corset wearer is always the submissive, the slave," writes Stephanie Jones. But this is not true; the symbolism of the corset is more complex. Some sadomasochists believe that leather corsets are only for dominants and rubber corsets only for submissives, but others insist that corsets have no such "predetermined sexual 'colour.'" The meaning of the corset is contextual and constructed: "The dominatrix wears her corset as armour, its extreme and rigid curvature the ultimate sexual taunt at the slave who may look but not touch.... The slave, on the other hand, is corseted as punishment."[15] The corseted dominatrix looks and feels "impenetrable." By contrast, the corset for the slave both signifies and enforces a sense of "discipline" and "bondage." Because of this, the corset is often used in "the transformation of male into she-male." It simultaneously gratifies his wish to look like a woman, while punishing him and thus assuaging his sense of guilt.[16]

The erotic appeal of the corset may be related to "the mystery of woman," suggests sex worker Alexis DeVille. "All I know is if I wear a corset in a scene, it gets better results with a slave than if I'm not wearing it."[17] For "masochists," on the other hand, "Even a moderately laced corset has a marvellously negative effect on the mobility, balance, and physical stability of its wearer." An article by Fakir Musafar on safe corseting techniques for sadomasochists emphasizes, however, that "a corset is a piece of equipment, with safety and quality requirements, just like many other pieces of SM equipment.... There are a few cautions to observe when doing SM scenes with tight corsets."[18]

Neither the word "slave" nor "sadomasochist" occurs in the nineteenth-century fetish literature, but many of the *EDM* letters contain references to "discipline," "confinement," "compulsion," "suffering," "pain," "torture," "agony," "submission," and "the victim." A small waist size alone was not enough for some

correspondents, who argued that "half the charm of a small waist comes, not in spite of, but on account of its being tight-laced" – "the tighter the better." "Well-applied restraint is in itself attractive."[19] (This was *extremely* unusual within the wider Victorian culture, where the "naturally" small waist was greatly preferred to its corseted facsimile.)

Some votaries, like Alfred, sadistically imagined female victims: *"There is something to me extraordinarily fascinating in the thought that a young girl has for many years been subjected to the strictest discipline of the corset. If she has suffered, as I have no doubt she has, great pain... from their extreme pressure, it must be quite made up to her by the admiration her figure excites."*[20]

But it was also common for correspondents to imagine men and boys who were forced to tight-lace at the hands of dominant women. Others were inspired to torture and victimize themselves. One man wrote to *Modern Society* in 1909, "I was persuaded... to get a pair of corsets by a 'Tortured Victim' with a waist of seventeen inches."[21]

Krafft-Ebing described one man who enjoyed the "pain of tight-lacing, experienced by himself or induced in women."[22] Wilhelm Stekel, another major sexologist writing in the early twentieth century, described several such cases, including a "respectable" married man who tight-laced, cross-dressed, and wore women's high-heeled shoes that were so tight that he limped. "It actually appeared as if physical pain were an integral part of his bliss and he gloated in it as long as it were caused by some feminine article of apparel." He had also "collected all the literature that had been written for and against [tight-lacing]. He often tried to lace himself so tightly that he would faint but in this he was unsuccessful. He even succeeded in persuading his wife to lace herself closely and tied her corset tighter every day himself until her waistline had been reduced about six inches. This also gratified him sexually."[23]

A 36-year-old policeman who consulted Stekel also wore corsets and "masturbate[d] before a mirror with the fantasy that he is the woman he saw." The policeman had filled a scrapbook with pictures of corsets clipped from newspapers and overlaid with obscene sketches and marginal notes: "Ha! what a thrill to disrobe such an insanely corseted woman and then rape her (first her corset would split in the struggle)." Stekel refers to this volume as the fetishist's "Bible," and draws attention to the contrast between the man's Christian and celibate life and his "hellish" fantasies.[24]

Pain and compression were frequently juxtaposed in the *EDM* letters with references to the "fascinating," "delightful," "delicious," "superb," "exquisite," and "pleasurable" sensations supposedly afforded by tight-lacing. Pain and pleasure were not the only issues, however. Dominance and submission were at least as important. Hence the many stories about forced tight-lacing.

1 Michel Foucault, Discipline and Punish: The Birth of the Prison, trans. Alan Sheridan (New York: Vintage Books, 1979), pp. 138, 25.

2 See Steele, Fashion and Eroticism, Chapter 9: "The Corset Controversy."

3 Rigid corsets with whalebone stays first appeared in sixteenth-century Europe. The iron "corsets" of the same period were not the fashion, but rather were crude orthopedic instruments intended to correct spinal deformations. Erotic enthusiasm bega to focus on the corset in the eighteenth century, and spread rapidly in the later nineteenth century – the same pattern we see with shoe fetishism.

4 Susan Faludi, Backlash: The Undeclared War Against American Women (New York: Crown, 1991), p. 189

5 Faludi, Backlash, p. 173

6 Ibid., pp. 496 and 499.

7 Moralist, EDM (February, 1871), p. 127.

8 V. Vale and Andrea Juno, eds., Modern Primitives (San Francisco: Re/Search Publications, 1989), pp. 29-30.

9 Hyygeia, "Does Tight-Lacing Really Exist?" The Family Doctor (September 3, 1887), p. 7

10 "Tight-Lacing," The Family Doctor (March 3, 1888), p. 1.

11 Measurements of corsets in other museum collections indicate that the majority were 20 to 26 inches when laced completely closed – and many women left their corsets open in back two or three inches. See Chapter 9 of Fashion and Eroticism for a further analysis of corset and dress measurements.

12 Mistress Angel Stern, "A 'Corset Moment' with Pearl," Verbal Abuse Number 3: New Religions (1994), p. 7.

13 Modern Primitives, pp. 15, 8.

14 Fakir Musafar, quoted in Gloria Brame, William Brame, and Jon Jacobs, Different Loving (New York: Villard, 1994), p. 311

15 tephanie Jones, "Strictly Fashionable: A Straight-Laced Look at Corsetry," Skin Two, Number 9, pp. 45-47.

16 Ibid.

17 Alexis DeVille interview, in Brame, et al., Different Loving, p. 319.

18 Fakir Musafar, "The Corset and Sadomasochism," Sandmutopia Guardian: A Dungeon Journal (issue 11), n.d., pp. 14-16.

19 See, for example, La Genie, EDM (September 1868), p. 166. There is further discussion of this issue in Fashion and Eroticism.

20 Alfred, EDM (January 1871), p. 62.

21 Modern Society (December 25, 1909), p. 22.

22 Krafft-Ebing, p. 253.

23 William Stekel, Sexual Aberrations: The Phenomenon of Fetishism in Relation to Sex (New York: Horace Liveright, 1930), vol. 1, pp. 222-224.

24 Stekel, vol. 1, pp. 218-220.

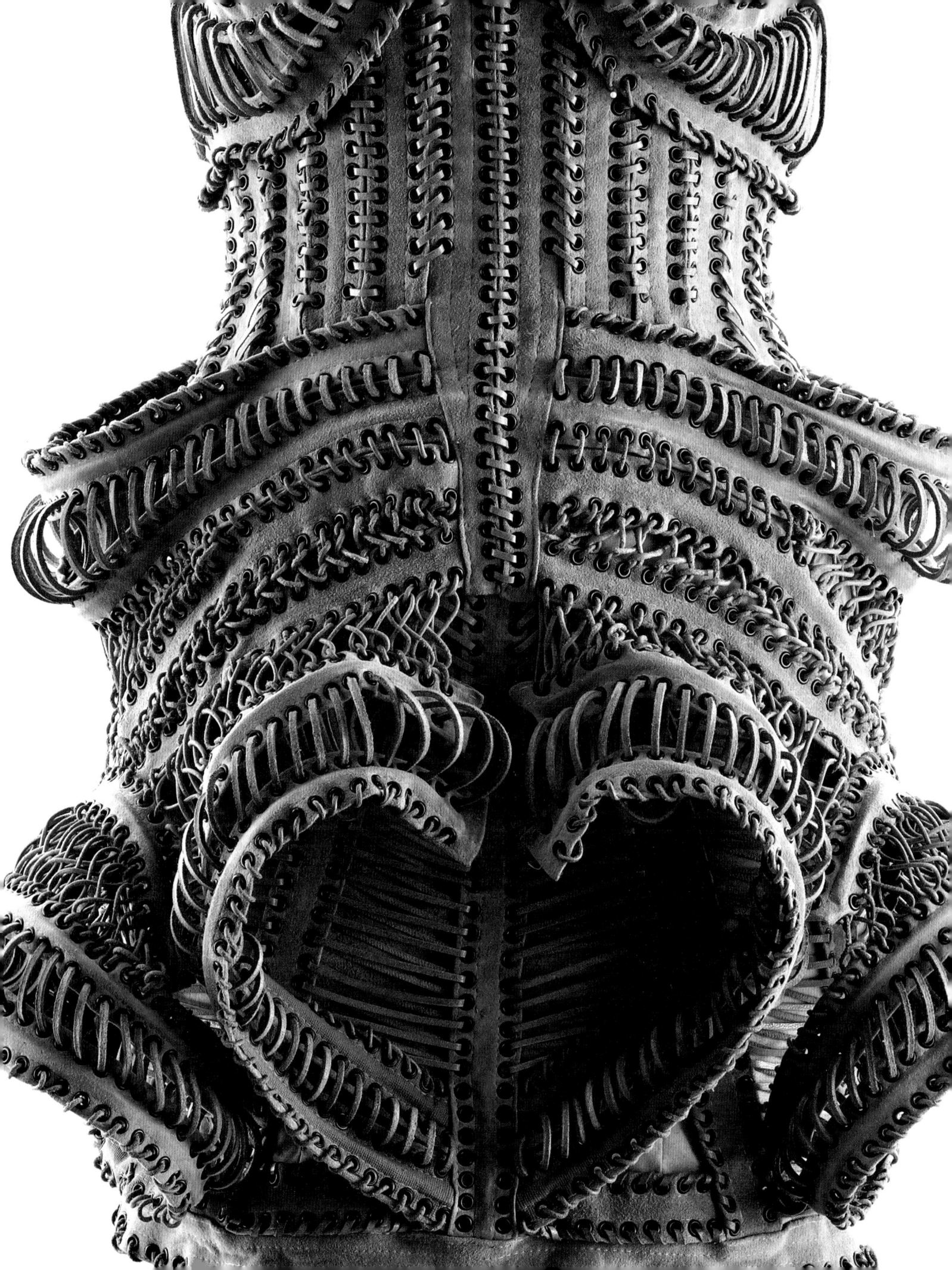

The Eye of the Storm

BY LIDEWIJ EDELKOORT

Her parents made the perfect choice, she absolutely inhabits her given name. She is as magical and full of mystery as the colour and texture of her eye, of our eyes, the iris. The iris is the peripheral element that structures and contains the pupil like a sphincter and filters light like a cell. It is slightly ruffled at the edges like a textile, able to fold like paper, iridescent like a laser, concentrated like a lens, engineered like a futuristic material...

If beauty is in the eye of the beholder, our eyes should recognise the intriguing similarity between the creations of Iris van Herpen and the inner workings of the iris. Enhancing and dilating colour and structure by using optical illusions. She moulds, folds and projects form, she lends from the organic to create the futuristic and even sometimes the absurdist. Her inspirations are within the realm of the fantastic and the biological, a hybrid of elegant yet cutting-edge couture. Since the brain can only perceive the layering of two dimensions, she uses 3D printing to suggest volume, teaching the eye to see.

Her vision for our future is full of enigma. Proposing restraining corseted dresses that allow us to feel contained and go beyond ourselves. She will further use the newest technologies to produce coverings and to engineer elegance. A quest for projecting and understanding our times. Her designs forecast the aura of a new day. Valerie Steele is right to describe her as "one of the most innovative and exciting fashion designers working today."

Manimal:
What if they are like us?

BY JEFF RIAN

PHOTOGRAPHY BY CHRISTOPH THEURER

Anyone who has studied animals will tell you that they communicate and can be cantankerous and snooty just like Fifi is when she's hungry or wants to go out. The most notable is the case of Washoe, a chimpanzee who in the late 1960s learned 130 hand signs of the American Language of the deaf. (Many others have learned it since.) Others seem to emote.

Whales and elephants utter tones too low for us to hear and are noted to hover around a conspecific in distress. Primates such as chimpanzees suffer from grief and loneliness particularly when a mate or kin is killed. Pigs scream and cows wrench in anxiety when they sense their slaughter. Sterile worker ants even commit suicide. Captive animals often refuse food, wither and die, as if by intention.

Many animas kill their own or another's offspring in struggles over power. A male lion who has overtaken a pride will kill the vanquished male's offspring so the females will ovulate to induce reproduction with the new dominating Alpha male. Animals also seem to exhibit jealousy, tenderness, anger and duplicity, which suggests complex "feelings", but they might not be the same love or hatred or revenge as ours. Nor do they feel future anxiety, nostalgia, Platonic love, or the beauty of the sublime, which Dionysus Longinus and Arthur Schopenhauer described as a mix of awe and terror, and William Blake exemplified in the 'fearful symmetry' of his 'tiger burning bright.'

Perhaps it is simply because animals lack opposable thumbs and labial speech that large-brained mammals like dolphins and elephants have failed to converse or sulk like brooding Hamlets or spend their lives glorifying the psychology of intensity, as did Nietzsche. A quirk of physical evolution makes us different — but not so different that we don't teach our children to stand up for themselves, be aggressive, stop whining, turn the other cheek, then take an eye for an eye. We describe each other as doves or hawks, lambs or tigers, chickens or wolves. And depending on the context, we demand both.

In folklore and classical mythology, our multifaceted personality is expressed in animal symbolism. Depictions convey our affinity for animal power across time, from the bison petrographs of the Lascaux Cave to leopard-print tights by Roberto Cavalli. Satyrs with horse bodies, Minotaur men with bull's heads, Satan emerging from the underworld in the guise of a snake, and angels guarding the heavens. The trickster Coyote plays the role of the Amerindian's Hermes, the prankster messenger of the gods, offering the wisdom of the ages and tips on behaviour. We call each other snake, pig, lion and monkey to describe our duplicity, slovenliness, magnetism, and foolishness. Armchair warriors urge on the ceremonial combat of Tigers or Dolphins and decorate their dens with growling throw rugs, carry rabbits' feet on a keychain for good luck, and hang raccoon tails from a car antenna. Animals and animal images decorate most all of our ephemera in one way or another and convey a latent cosmic purpose: to bring us closer to the animals – our vertebrate kin. They symbolize emotions we attribute to our 'natural' but otherwise culture-clad selves.

From childhood on, stories and metaphors abound with noble beasts. The kingly lion, showy peacock, wise elephant, duplicitous snake, peaceful dove, and grand soaring eagle of coins reveal something about our sense of style, and how we gussy up power and aggression in order to tame that tiger. The animal intensity of a 'fox' in D&G tiger skin or a stallion in a Gucci pony jacket synthesizes the paradox of animal passion and sophistication. Fashion draws out our sensitivity, while allowing us the subtle aggression necessary to optimize our mating capacity. So as superficial as fashion is supposed to be, it consumes us and highlights the paradox of aesthetic sensitivity and animal aggression that makes us hot.

Socially we speak of acting "naturally", but are reprimanded for waking up on the wrong side of the bed or for being moody when our blood sugar is low. Animals exhibit moodiness, but it's we who are grumpy as bears. And when we say our cat is acting just like our dog, what we mean is he is acting as if he is as domesticated as a dog. Moreover, "natural" is meaningless, because we can't really act otherwise. There is, however, a puppy dog side that animals exhibit and that we cling to particularly in regressive states. As children we cuddle our stuffed bunny, and as adults we

favour our pets over our mates. Perhaps these are retrogressive or doting paternal states that are activated when we're overcome with tender feelings or when we feel relaxed and floppy. And as far altruism goes, even animals have been seen rescuing a non-conspecific's offspring – elephants have been witnessed aiding a rhino calf, also chimpanzees rescuing a baby chick. And though at war, it is mostly humans who are incited to rage and revenge, resulting in violent murderous acts.

We say we work like dogs, are busy as a beaver, slave like an ant, eat like a bear, pursue like a fox. Such descriptions really trace back to the bridge we have long created between them and ourselves. The personality we inscribe onto Princess or Spot really documents the degree to which we have domesticated ourselves. As Jeffrey Masson and Susan McCarthy ask in their book, When Elephants Weep (Vintage, 1996), can it be the other way? When a cat offers a dead bird to its owner – its version of the Alpha male – is it being "zoomorphic"? Are they imposing their "cat" feelings onto us? Or, as the writers suggest, are animals as complicated in their behaviour as we are in our moods?

In every way we are kin to the animals, except in our culture, of which they are subjects so low that most are simply a food group. For in overcoming Nature we consumed it. The Ancestral Amerindians who made their way from Asia to the Americas ate an entire species of bison. Between 1830 and 1895 the American buffalo population was reduced from 70 million to 800, simply to subdue the "savage" Indian population who lived off them. President Theodore Roosevelt, a renowned Great White Hunter, compared the American grizzly bear's timidity and ferocity to a man's; but he could not refrain from killing every one he saw.

An innate yin-yang schizophrenia inheres to those puppy dog caresses and ghoulish moods. Often we pet our animals simply to assuage hostility to alienation that we might be feeling. Yet the Dionysian side of behavioural intensity is considered to be inherently savage – or animal, while the turn-the-other-cheek humility of a cuckold like St. Joseph, the generosity of Mother Teresa, or the bosomy kindness of the Tooth Fairy, are manifestations of culture and breeding. Culture is constructed around these paradoxes. It's goal is to breed out the gore with its written and unwritten laws, while clothing, architecture, religion, and art dress up those higher principles of morality and beauty.

In The Moral Animal (Random House, 1994) Robert Wright examines animal and human behaviour from the perspective of 'the new science of evolutionary psychology', which explores behaviour through the lens of socio-biology, or ecology, Darwinian anthropology, and evolutionary psychology as it is also called. As his title suggests, the paradox of being human lies in the fact

we are animals that use morality to assist our survival. Weaving his study of evolutionary psychology with a biographical sketch of the life of Charles Darwin – an exemplar of social reticence – Wright offers the story of how humility can be a form of passive aggression, particularly when articulated through the complexities of politeness. Darwin had thoroughly documented but had not yet published his theory of natural selection – which he'd been worrying over for twenty years. Then one day, he received a paper Alfred Russel Wallace had been circulating, whom he knew well and was on friendly terms, which discussed the same theory. Darwin then played the shrinking violet and deferred to friends and fellow-scientists Charles Lyell and Joseph Hooker to decide who should be given credit. By putting the decision into the laps of friends, true or not, his passive manipulation resulted in natural selection's being named after Darwin, not Wallace.

This is our animal side, too. For we use morality, laws, art, and religion to hold us in check. And though we no longer scrawl bison on cave walls to invoke dinner to saunter our way, we accept rage, shame and humility as integral elements of our complex personalities. We also call upon the savage muses in fashion, sports and seduction, and we use humility, moral indignation and even submission to mask our self-interest.

The closer we physically are to animals, however, the more easily we might attribute feelings of consciousness to parrots that talk, purpose to a dog that fetches his leash, learning to dolphins that improvise a performance, and sadness or mourning to elephants that cry. When we call "Barney!" and our basset hound comes smiling up, tail-wagging – or sulking with tail between legs – one has to wonder if he might think after all. And how bad will we feel if one day we find out he does?

It's unlikely that science will discover the key to human paradox or invent a pill to make everyone altruistic and gentle – and just as unlikely that such a revelation will stop us from calling each other bitch or bastard or chicken. Nor will we cease to revile behaviour that animals frolic in or desist from hushing those bursts of bodily emission we call uncouth.

Missionaries and anthropologists agree that you can't teach a naked man to read. By all historical evidence "high culture" requires more than just metaphysical cover up to accoutre and prolong itself. Aristotle first conceived of life as a plenitude of beings descending in perfect increments from the gods, to men, right on down to the amoebae.

We were God's subordinates, the animals were ours. Darwin first suggested that single-cell creatures were the prototypes for higher animals, including ourselves, thus turning Aristotle's Great Chain of Being upside down – i.e. higher creatures evolved from lower ones (God's starter kits). We owed something to them, after all. What's worse, in all likelihood they will outlast us. Darwin's Theory of Evolution also contained the seeds of today's evolutionary psychology – as well as the growing recognition that animals are not as insensitive as we thought. Fish do feel pain. Dogs and elephants and primates do suffer when they are separated from siblings.

The Arctic explorer Peter Freuchen wrote about Inuits leaving the elderly to die in enclosed igloos, eating their dogs, and even hanging their own children in times of starvation. These were gentle and warm people, he wrote, who felt deeply for children and the elderly but had no time (often literally) for sentimentality – something we moderns see as proliferating in the 18th century, along with the pornography industry.

In the movie *Planet of the Apes*, evolved primates cage dim-witted humans in zoos. Then along come a few extra-terrestrial humans, who return by accident to Earth only to witness their past folly. The moral is that humans were the only creatures who could dramatically alter the number and population of different species, including their own. It's also likely that after the last wild animal has been tamed or placed in a zoo, we will still look at it and wonder, what if...

The Secret of the Apron

BY DOMINIQUE FALLECKER
PHOTOGRAPHY BY MARIE TAILLEFER

The apron is the most fascinating, dizzying, amazing, crazy garment ever created. It has been seen on everyone from Adam, Eve and the Serpent to prehistoric men and archaic ploughmen, Egyptian gods and the mischievous Knossos snake goddesses in Crete. Millennium after millennium, it thrives on this Earth. It is not a simple coincidence that Satan wears a leather apron either.

The apron is perverse and ambiguous. It "flouts the conventions" of morality, countries, and fashion. Greater than the Triple Hecate, it has a thousand faces. It can be divinely bad, malicious, sectarian, and depraved.

Despite being associated with an image of motherhood in popular culture, the apron is also a redeemer of women. Deprived of having a soul until the Council of Mason declared it otherwise in 825, the young maiden that on one hand symbolised purity was considered worthy to become a housewife. Dressed in her apron, she was charged with domestic chores and became part of society, giving birth, keeping house, feeding her family and obtaining the right to survive. At the same time, she remained dubious or even impure, thanks to her biological connection to nature's cycles, the sexuality she omitted and her beauty. Vulnerable and diabolical, she could even be transformed into a witch. In the north of Europe, the female apron was seen as a symbol of protection against bad forces, deflecting harm away from the household.

The apron soon encountered everybody: Jack the Ripper and good schoolboys, soldiers, workers, elegant women, and even Balenciaga who raised it to an art. The apron is universal; always evolving, but maintaining its primitive shape – a body with ties, perhaps a bib and a yoke. It protects clothing from wear and tear, it covers the wearer from the waist down, leaving the back open except for the knotted ties. Professional or damned soul of the housewife, inseparable childhood friend or partner in erotic games, the apron has been fashioned from every material; from chain mail to paper, it can be a performer in the dirtiest sense or an emblem of *coquetterie*.

A conspicuous sign of wealth and power, and indissociable from costume history, the apron was layered over common garments such as skirts and petticoats, providing a visual code that connected an individual to a particular professional or social caste. The royal Spanish court's etiquette declared that the apron, a narrow rectangle of silk, be worn with court dresses. And very often aprons can form part of a wealthy bride's dowry, such as in the legendary and luxurious twenty aprons of a Danish princess. Yet while the apron strutted around palaces, it also hid in grimy holes and corners of the city streets, where it covered beggars' shapeless rags.

Far from the dreams, glories and sorrows of the old days, the apron scoffed, seeing falsely virtuous women looking moral in it, as a suggestive symbol of motherhood; worn to cuddle children and provide them refuge against fear, but also to punish boys by "pinaforing" – dressing a boy in a girl's clothing – perhaps because they had always longed for a daughter, or found it fitting to feminize their sons. This phenomenon may also have been seen in marital relationships, where women exerted control over their husbands by forcing them to wear a feminine apron, printed with flowers and trimmed with flounces and ribbons.

Able to quickly forget this depravity, the apron also enjoyed a life in Haute Couture. Celebrated for and taking pleasure in its beauty, twinkling on the catwalk and reflecting light like pearls of dew, a mist of silk.

The apron nevertheless also became a fragile feminine armour when rumours of war spread throughout the world as in the 1930s, when the apron dress was at the height of fashion. Needless to say, it's perhaps better not to mention what happened after the war, when such extraordinary connotations were over and when women had to go back to "normalcy," again finding their home life as a domestic servant.

Also ambiguous on the silver screen, the apron sometimes shares the spotlight with fairy tale stars in Walt Disney movies or in the *Wizard of Oz* where a blue version became as famous as its wearer Judy Garland, and a star in its own right. In *The Man Who Shot Liberty Valence* it symbolized the paradoxical values for which Ransom Stoddard fights: the brave code of ethics which leads him to sacrifice and which simultaneously grows out of the darkest and most feminine part of him. Or the apron appears more simply in *Scarlet Street*, which depicts the pinaforing of a man, feminized and powerless because he is shown wearing an obviously womanly apron.

The apron is also a code which lets one distinguish quickly between the person who is wearing an apron and the person who has none.

APRON FETISH

The hierarchy is thus established; the relationship between the inferior and the superior, the domestic and the master, and also among the servants and the various maids, with the governess at the top of the hierarchy wearing no apron.

Like a coat of arms for the bourgeois and the bohemian, the apron was the star of the organic Sunday lunch, the crowning moment of the week. Back on a farm for only a weekend, in the middle of nowhere, straw hat on the head, collarless shirts for men and long skirts for women, Swedish clogs in bright colours placed in front of the door for decoration – the apron worked with them to cook garden tomatoes, tiny sour apples and collect eggs from rare breed hens; from the meadows to the kitchen in its vast and unforgettable folds.

Meanwhile, in Paris, in the kitchens of beautiful apartments in the city's best districts, the host or hostess, wrapped in a spotless white apron with his or her hand-embroidered first name, prepared Sunday dinner for a few happy guests.

Trying to define the apron is an impossible task because it is always found where no one is looking for it; for example, as a garment of meditation and peace in Masonic lodges. For the Freemasons, the apron was a medium that went from the secular world to the lodge's sacred space – it gave them the ability to receive and pass on the initiation. It was an important emblem of Masonic beliefs, covering the part of the body where passions come to life, to tame them, and also the visual code to differentiate apprentices from companions, masters, and the venerable; a way of marking the characteristics of each rank.

Universal or regional, but never national, the apron in its various infinite and adaptable forms federates otherwise improbable elements and is a symbol of identity in folkloric costume; all the while maintaining its pulse on real life and evolving with the times. While its form may remain similar, its ornamentation offers a multitude of possibilities and facets, including the horizontal folding of traditional aprons from Marken, a former isle in the Ijsselmeer, the Netherlands, which unfold like an intricate origami.

But the apron is perhaps, above all, a fetishistic tease. Viewed from the front, it covers almost everything, but from the back, the imagination is free to fantasize about its sudden lack of fabric. Hypocritically appearing as a baby's bib, it is the secret fetish of infantilists, worshippers of nannies, aprons, and diapers, and (with or without kitchen towels), the totem of *podiaphilie*.[1]

It is true that the apron protects and connects, but it does so with great ambiguity. It is constantly shifting its form. It is a free electron in a rigidly formatted world. Professional garment for some, fetish object for others, it is even more iconic than the little black dress, jeans, or the white T-shirt, because it is more elusive. But it does not matter because the apron can be dazzling or destroyed, tied with its knot in the back – it will always be an indisputable expression of freedom or desire.

---

1   A French term signifying a fetish for kitchen aprons, blouses and dish towels.

Braided Love

BY DR SUSANNE PIËT

What is it with braids or plaits? In an era when it is important to stand out and state your identity as an instrument of success worth more than money or heritage because it creates attention and reputation. And Yes: hair in general, and the braid in particular, can do that.

What is it with braids or plaits? In an era when it is important to stand out and state your identity as an instrument of success, it's worth more than money or heritage and creates attention and reputation. And Yes: hair in general, and the braid in particular, can do that.

The braid can be emblematic and act like a personal brand. Think of Yulia Tymoshenko whose hair-crowned beauty marked her role in the Orange Revolution of 2004, bringing down the post-Soviet government in Kiev. I remember an image in which she, then prime minister, not haphazardly dressed in a gown with lace gloves, offers her hand to be kissed by the president. Her braid in traditional Ukrainian style was certainly a calculated political tool with significant cultural resonance. To her supporters she thus became Lady Liberty.

The braid itself became fashion. The American singer Beyoncé appeared with an equally appealing (blond) plaited crown around that time. And we saw Janet Jackson and Rihanna with plaits too. Another emblematic appearance was offered by the Mexican artist Frida Kahlo. Her fame cannot be separated from the image of her long or built up plaits; that frame or crown, her stern look with the black connected eyebrows. That's become her thing so to speak. Plaits can be your thing too, your brand. Also now, while I write, long hair and especially the loose plait is prominently in fashion. But it can be more. It can be a fetish.

Human History of Hair

How nice it is to look at girls in school uniforms with plaited hair. Or older adolescent girls in loosely plaited hair (*La Fille aux Cheveux de Lin*, Claude Debussy), or dark girls with a thousand braids around their beautiful shiny laughing faces. So innocent, so neat, so fresh, so organized in a way. A hairstyle uncomplicated. Yet refined. Innocent and purposeful. Chastity and sensuality. Confusing? The braid can exert an appealing mixture of emotional influence: sensual and sexual. It's probably because religion is seldom naive that the braid has been forbidden in the bible, especially, as I found, in Timothy 2:9-10.

It's text implies that you can use the braid as a device to stick jewels in, something that has been done by ancient Greeks and wealthy women in the Renaissance, as many sculptures and portraits show. All through human existence people have braided hair, especially head hair. I mention the Himbas (saw them for myself on my visit to Namibia and Botswana). Beautiful. The Yoruba's in South West Nigeria have created architectural braid-wonders on the heads of girls. The Chiribyani in Mexico reserved the plaiting technique not only for girls; men also braided their hair, and the technique served as a weapon against lice. And of course even as a child, I associated plaits with emblems of communities. All Chinese people had one on their back in my mind and American Indians always had two plaits, a conviction I thank not so much to cultural anthropologists as to illustrators of books and graphic novels.

Food for Fetishists

In the recently reopened Rijksmuseum in Amsterdam – where not only has the building been renovated, but the concept of historical storytelling has also been rethought – the Dutch middle ages have been eye marked by a strange and remarkable object protected in a glass showcase. It is a blond plait attributed to Jacoba van Beieren (1401-1436); the plait as a relic. It must have been cut off before her burial, and the action of cutting, saving and honouring hair, especially plaits or braids of the deceased, has been a thing for many purposes, including the following three:

• First: the plait or braid as a memory, often contained in mourning jewellery. This became high fashion after the death of the English Prince Albert in 1861 when Queen Victoria set this trend in her mourning attire. Since then, Victorian mourning adornments have become highly collectable. In the United States, it was customary for women who stayed behind while their husbands went to fight in the Civil War to keep at least a piece of their hair in a locket or other piece of jewellery.

• Second: hair as a piece of victory, in casu the scalp. Imagine a soldier savagely cutting a crown off the head by the hair, before lifting it in the air triumphantly to show it to his combatants. Those scalps became a totem, according to scientist John Frazer in 1910: an object considered with superstitious respect, since it is believed to protect the clan from further danger. Another example is the piece of braid collected by the (serial) killer or the obsessional rapist.

• Third: hair, the braid or the plait in particular as a sexual fetish.

Though I have plaited my long hair in various stages throughout life and in different variations (also the Frida Kahlo way, eliciting questions like "Are you an Indian by the way?"), I have never though of my hair as a possible fetish or as an offering to fetishists. How naive I was: of course: Hair in general is a fetishistic item and the plait or braid in particular! Apart from the schoolgirl fantasy, there is the whip association, and maybe more. Everybody knows that now thanks to the upsurge of erotic fantasies in every shade of grey and the tsunami of similar books thereafter. What was I thinking?

Hair fetishism has other names as well: "hair partialism" is one, but "trichophilia" is even better, as it consists of the Greek words for "hair" and "love." Arousal by head hair may arise from seeing, touching or smelling long or short hair, wet hair, a certain colour of hair or a particular hairstyle. The erotic hair-love or obsession finds its ground in the fact that the perception of hair awakens certain parts of the brain to activate sex hormones via pheromones. The olfactory, touchable and visible stimulus creates sexual arousal, sometimes with uncontrollable reactions in the fetishist.

A special yet alarming variation is the sexual preference in some amateurs for eating hair, (besides head hair, also pubic hair, and even that can be braided): food for fetishists indeed. A hair fetishist can be inventive with hair and one of their obsessions is specifically directed toward the braid or the plait. When styled so, the hair could resemble a whip to a certain extent. "Women can whip me with their hair: the ultimate turn-on," confided one man. The braid can come in handy as a handle, comfortable for at least one party in the sexual act. Men and also women can thoroughly enjoy pulling or even cutting a young girl's braid of hair. They may steal parts of braids, and interesting for the innocent walker, snip them off in pieces to disperse in public spaces. Such activities arouse them. Others may find the attraction of literally "having sex with somebody's hair" as a fantasy or fetish, which leaves a lot up to the imagination. This fetish affects both men and women.

Braid or Plait

I have used the terms braid and plait at random, but there is a subtle difference between a braid and a plait. In both cases the action to make them is interweaving or intertwining; an activity that can soothe and reorganize the mind. The distinction between the two varieties has to do with the intensity and the starting point. The braid has been defined as an interweaving for three or more strips of something, including textile or rope. Woven hair creates a very strong tool.

The plait is also the result of the intertwining of strands or strips in a pattern. The word is related to an old French term for plait that means "folding", as does the Latin "plicare." You can use this technique for ribbons or textiles as well. When it comes to hair, the braid is the variation where the interweaving starts tight to the skull, like in African tribal traditions or while grooming your horse. While with the plait, the interweaving starts lower and is usually also loose – as seen in Albrecht Dürer's painting *The Furlegerin* – plaiting does not have to be limited to head hair of course. In 2009, a "beard champion" wove a complete tapestry under his chin!

In Your Dreams...

Lots of people have hair dreams. Losing hair is a common topic and fear, difficult to discern from the fear of death. There are also recurrent dreams about braids; braided hair in your dream means, according to some dream interpreters, the subconscious recognition of childlike innocence and successful organization skills. It is true that the plait or braid represent a certain mixture of ingenuity, organisation, rhythm and playfulness.

While the mind can relax by braiding, the almost trancelike feeling is an experience every true horse-riding girl shares. This effect can be therapeutic. Who knows what we can build, create or design in an era where self-sufficiency and recycling become more and more useful and highly appreciated. At the Crystal Palace exhibition in 1853, an entire tea set of hair was on display, made by hair workers in Scandinavia. What more with hair is in stall for us? I have my hair dreams too...

Guinean Idol

BY PHILIP FIMMANO
PHOTOGRAPHY BY NAMSA LEUBA

The potent photographic lens of Namsa Leuba is one that reveals fresh perspectives of the ever-morphing African identity. In *Ya Kala Ben*, a series she created in her graduation year at ECAL, the Swiss-born artist, half-Guinean in heritage, travelled to Conakry to study the country's local rites and rituals. Leuba was indeed looking for something hard to attain, "interested in the construction and deconstruction of the body as well as the depiction of the invisible." The intriguing images formed part of a two-year investigation into the ideas and perceptions of Africa abroad.

In her photographs, Leuba re-appropriates the statuettes that are traditionally used in Guinean ceremonies and customs. Embedded with multiple layers of symbolism, the statuettes are considered powerful, known for possessing an innate cultural value through their very essence; yet by bringing these idols into the context of an on-location shoot that could as easily be destined for the pages of Vogue as for an art gallery's walls, Leuba has transformed her statuettes into contemporary icons.

But what of the styling, and what of the costume? By repositioning the "Africanness", Leuba played to preconceived expectations and appeased foreign tastes. Concurrently, she had to sometimes deal with violent reactions from Guineans who considered the practice a form of sacrilege; evidently "afraid and struck with astonishment."

The photographs have attracted much acclaim, including the 2012 Hyères PhotoGlobal Prize which led to further study at the School of Visual Arts in New York City. Leuba is currently preparing for a residency in South Africa as part of a grant from the Pro Helvetia Foundation.

What is perhaps most remarkable about her work is the promise of things to come. At a time when Africa is positioned as a new frontier, this photographer's oeuvre challenges old notions of place and traditions, while evoking and provoking new ones.

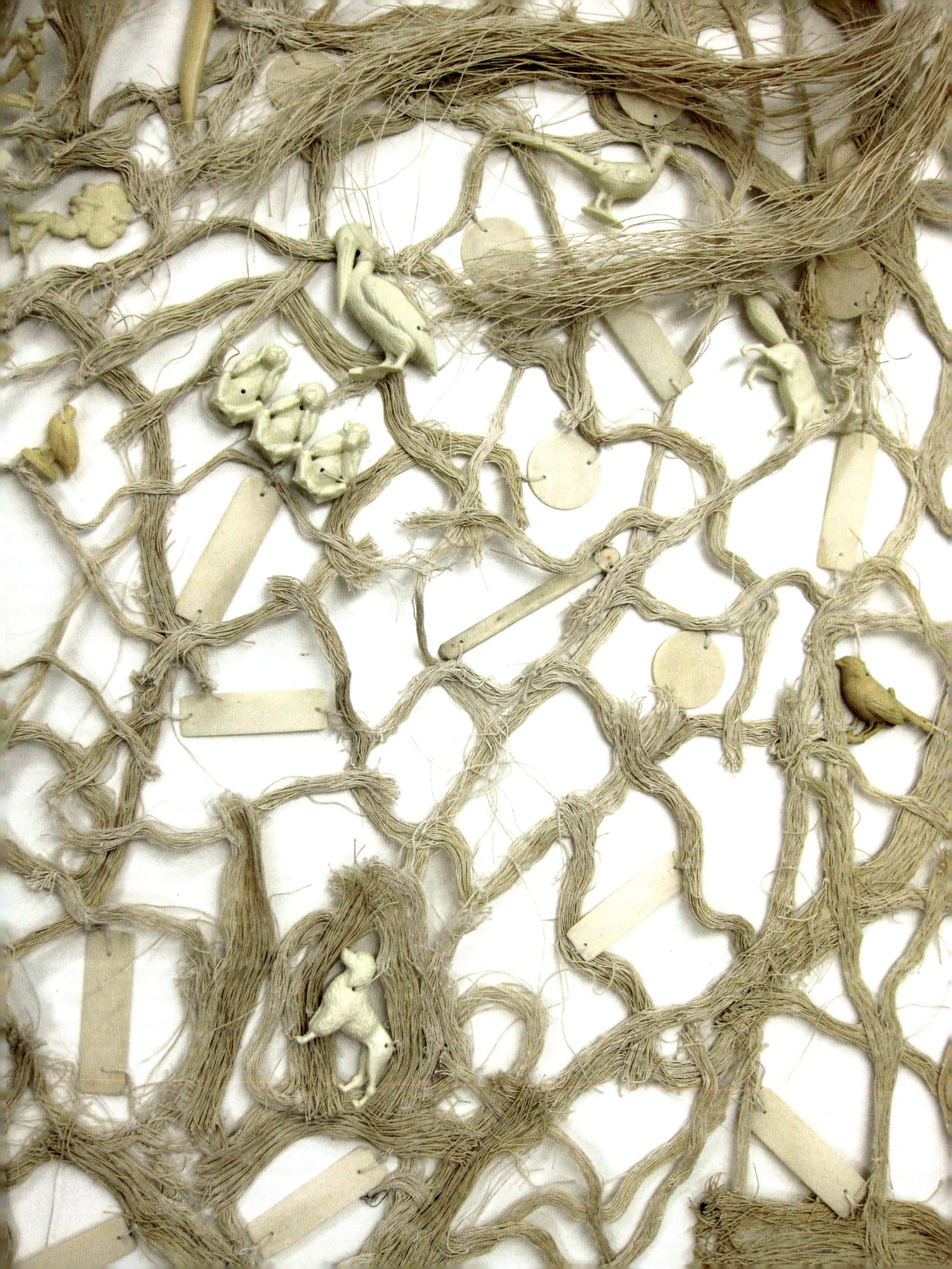

Subliminal Inspiration

BY KAREN NICOL

The treasure troves of inspiration in museums and galleries stimulate me as a mixed-media textile designer. I've always loved wandering about with a notebook scribbling down ideas of how I could interpret shapes, textures and patterns to try to take embroidery out of its predictable confines. Our imaginations are only as rich as their input, so continuous "feeding" is essential. For decades, my husband, collage artist Peter Clark and I have trawled flea markets and boot sales all over the world looking for the visual stimulus to be found in unwanted junk and our home is a constantly changing gallery.

My studio is like a frantic sketchbook page. I gather around me numerous collections of small, insignificant things, chosen in a magpie-like way. Put together, they begin to make palettes of "qualities" to inform the senses. I am passionate about these values. The dryness or the waxiness, the silkiness or the pitted roughness, the fragility or the simple form, rearranging them to react to different influences can give a constantly shifting vocabulary. Texture and tactility play such a significant part of the craft, it is important to keep stimulating these senses.

Subconsciously, I have been influenced again and again by my fetish for the collected paraphernalia in my archive. It is more like subliminal informing: seeing something with peripheral vision, like learning a language by listening to it in your sleep. My collections have had remarkable intuitive impact on my designs over the years.

Inspiration is not an insular thing. Physical and emotional properties from all around us cross-reference each other to bring an idea to life and make it contemporary. We can look at the same piece of inspiration at various times and take something totally different from it depending upon what else is affecting us visually. It is of no benefit to mindlessly copy. We have to add the magic of our own personal way of seeing with the absorption of all the intangible stimulus which influence our viewpoint.

Fashion is like a big intestine. It digests everything around us-art, music, politics, the social world to make a collection that people love. Because, without analysing it too much, we absorb our surroundings.
– Jean Paul Gaultier

It's a tricky thing starting art college at 17 and feeling desperate to be cool, to find that the subject you are instinctively best at is one that gets smirks of derision from your fine art and sculpture-studying contemporaries. I had to swallow my pride because I had discovered the huge breadth, excitement and potential in embroidery.

Thankfully now, in its new guises of mixed-media, multi-media or surface design, it is accepted that as well as spanning fashion, space, gallery and craft it can embrace all of textile embellishment that is not print, weave or knit. It can encompass any medium used on textiles or any textile technique used on other materials including painting, gluing, stapling, concrete, wood or stone and does not need to be bound by any of the rules of stitch, but it still has its stigma.

What is exceptional about embroidery is that you can use it with the same mark-making freedom as a painter uses a paintbrush, or a sculptor embraces form. We become "painters" with textures and qualities and there are a million different surfaces to play with. The more embroidery I do the more I realize is possible.

My work spans fashion, interiors and gallery but the motivation and design processes are all very similar. I love the freedom with gallery work to be able to explore three-dimensional pieces but the large animals I embroider I still see as creatures wearing couture fashion fabric skins. My embroideries for interiors also offer wonderful opportunities with size and repeat but I see the designs as clothing a room.

As a student at the Royal College of Art I fell in love with the fashion side of textiles, I thrived on the fast pace, the glamour and the opportunity for constant renewal and experimentation. The relationship between fashion and textiles is a wonderful collaboration.

It is a delicious cycle, cloth inspiring fashion and fashion inspiring cloth. The outward looking fashion designer sees the vision of the show, the story or theme behind the collection, the silhouette, the weight and the mood. The textile designer, also peering into the future, looks at the possibilities like an artist with his canvas, conjuring up a plethora of qualities and techniques, finishes and patterns in order to capture the intangible mood of the time, developing a textile which will help change a piece of cloth into the latest vision. Textiles can transform a silhouette or put substance to a dream as well as merely decorate.

The cut of a piece of clothing, whether complex or perfectly simple can have many hours invested in it to create the perfect pattern. This can then be made into a valuable asset when changed many times just by using different cloths. A simple, shaped garment already proven to look good and sell well can be transformed continuously season after season by different treatments with textiles.

Practically there are many different ways that fashion designers and textile artists work together; for instance, the fashion designer can choose from new collections of ready-produced fabric from textile fairs or buy designs straight from a textile portfolio and produce the fabric themselves.

I have been lucky enough to work freelance alongside fashion designers as part of the team of pattern cutters, printers and seamstresses. I create a series of samples informed by the ideas, colours, silhouettes and ground fabrics that have been chosen as the kernel of the collection, and yet still very influenced by my own research into technique and imagery.

I have often worked for many different people in the same season so interpretation of each designer's character and mood is essential as is the need for lateral thinking, copious ideas and a free-wheeling attitude to experimentation in the search for new ways of approaching the craft. There will often be a brief for a collection, which can be as simple as "we want something funky" or as rich and inspiring as the "Frida Khalo meets Singapore whorehouse" by Clements Ribeiro. Sometimes, often advantageously, the brief asks for the impossible stretching the limitations of embroidery into innovation.

Totems to Taste

BY PHILIP FIMMANO
DESIGN BY MA'AYAN PESACH

Our strongest memories can be related to feelings, experiences, places, events and objects. These emotions last a lifetime and can be awaked by a particular smell, appearance, tactility or sound. Food is of course a powerful instigator of such memories, and in the work of Ma'ayan Pesach, food is a tool that opens an instinctive door to nostalgia.

The Israeli-born graduate from the Design Academy Eindhoven sees food as a road leading to a place of safety and comfort. As part of her *Food Stories Come Alive* series, Pasach has created a dinner set that illustrates the origin of food in a primal and almost tribal way. Waste items from the industry, such as bones, hair and skin, are incorporated into post-fossil dishes and totemic tabletop. Pesach created tableware that brings out the essence of food and its ethnicity into our meals; these elements are used in a subtle way that is not unattractive but still makes us wonder about their origins. The final outcome is a collection of unique fetishist objects that are semi-practical, and at times, abstract and surreal. Linking the origin of the species to the species at the table, and forging a more respectful relationship between the hunter and the hunted.

Ties That Bind

BY LIDEWIJ EDELKOORT

PHOTOGRAPHY BY MARIE TAILLEFER

FLORAL FETISH

Man has often imagined the ties that bind us in physical and sometimes painful form. To wrap the object of desire is to own it and master it, if only for a momentary surge of pleasure. The act of bondage has therefore penetrated art and photography, and has recently influenced daring fashions and excessive lingerie seen at private behind-the-scenes dinners. The next step is imminent.

Now we will take a leap of faith from the bodily to the botanical, and bind our blooms into a new form of erotic bouquet. Flesh-coloured flowers are tied with fine rope or skin-like rubber bands to subvert their aesthetics and forever transform ideas about the perfect gift. To adorn with fastenings – done up, then undone again – all the better to clasp and entwine each other. Sending a subliminal hint of things to come to the amorous receiver.

Anonymous & Veiled

BY PHILIP FIMMANO
PHOTOGRAPHY BY DAMSELFRAU

The Internet has been providing us with a veil of anonymity. We are now able to write under another name, to farm as a fictive person, to date as an incognito being, to behave like a foreigner or simply become a code. Its far-reaching influence brings out the other in us; we give in to our multiple personalities and experience the freedom of not being seen or heard.

Now spilling over into the real world, this phenomenon has become counterbalanced by a need for discretion; no doubt as a reaction against visual information overload, the reality TV syndrome and red carpet obsessions. Current fashions forecast a new period in which people will go undercover.

Like ghosts or clouds, we will suddenly materialise in urban life: dressed in colour, covered in textile, and moving in transparencies that play hide and seek. Ethnic and religious differences will be put aside, yet these beings will belong to another kind of chastity and privacy, dressed to disappear. Masked and covered, people will go through life behind a veil; very visible yet very discrete also. A strange need to feel and breathe textile is related to this movement, as is the wish to be disconnected from the world.

The remarkable work of Magnhild Kennedy forms part of this masked moment. Under the guise of her pseudonym Damselfrau (meaning 'maiden wife' in German), the self-taught designer produces accessories that are in intricately embroidered, meticulously beaded and poetically painted in her London studio. She works in an intuitive way, without sketches or advanced planning, and describes her fetish for materials as "compulsive". Damselfrau's masks are layered in history and meaning, crafted from textile shreds from far away places: a lock of hair from a Japanese geisha's headpiece, vintage laces from her native Norway, glass bead remnants from French Christmas ornaments...

Once her pieces are completed, Damselfrau gives the masks a name and posts photographs of herself wearing them on her blog, Twitter and Facebook (she considers them finished only once these images are placed online). The masks' naming process is an intrinsic step in her work; reinventing foreign words, updating Latin references, changing the spelling of a god or imagining a new mythical being. Sometimes the names is based on phonetics − "Is the piece more of an I, an O or a T?" − and sometimes ideas come from a recently-read book, such as the ancient Sanskrit text *Bhagavad Gita* which inspired the creation of an entire mask collection based on the beauty of its language

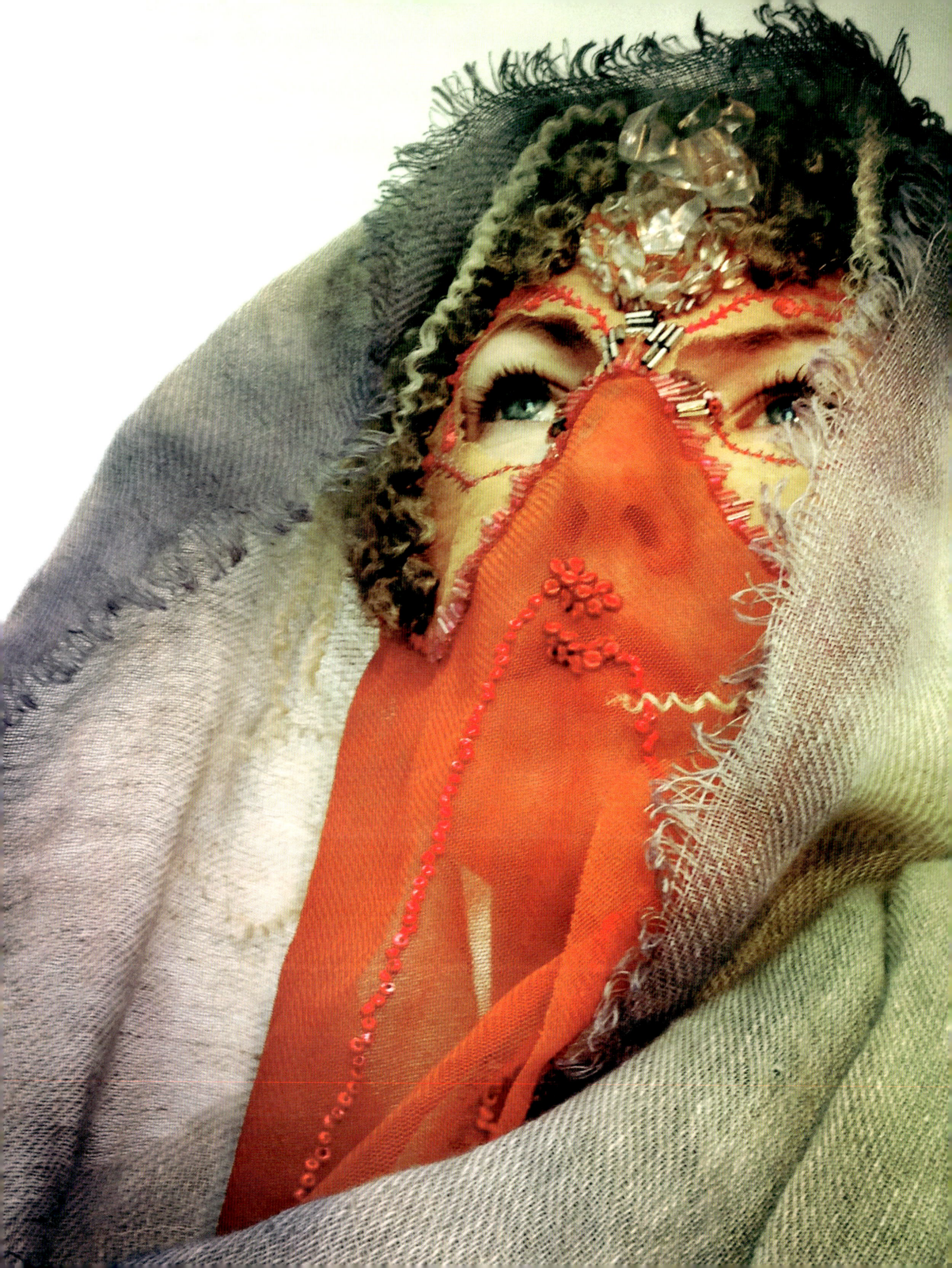

No Sex Please, We're Syrian: Confessions from the Lingerie Drawer

BY MALU HALASA
PHOTOGRAPHY BY GILBERT HAGE

A dramatic reappraisal of sex and sexual matters by Syria's younger generation of activists has swept the country since the uprising. Ordinarily before 2011, twenty-something Muslims used euphemisms to vent their frustrations. Derogatory words were not considered polite or acceptable language in a traditional society that was so firmly anchored by family and honour. Now social media has provided a platform to air more explicit views. Recently, one young Syrian wrote "dick bitch" twenty times on his Facebook page and then added: "Now do I have your attention? Four-hundred people died in Syria today."

For some, sex has become one way to deal with the violence around them, according to a 29-year-old woman journalist and activist who asked not to be identified. "A lot of people's relationships have collapsed and new relationships have begun," observed Laila (a pseudonym). "As a generation we used to be obsessed with what people were doing or what they thought. With so many depressed, imprisoned or dead since the beginning of the revolution, it's understandable that many people are moving to the extreme."

As much as some Syrian activists have been able to express themselves, in the frontline of the political battle, sex has been used to undermine public figures. Last year a photograph of a woman posing in skimpy lingerie, with her back to the camera, was included in a cache of hacked emails allegedly belonging to president Bashar Al-Assad. The woman, later identified by activists as presidential aide Hadeel Ali, was responsible for coining Assad's new nickname *bataa* ("duck" in Arabic) to great hilarity among internet pranksters. The authorities too were not above a dirty tricks campaign and released an embarrassing private Skype conversation between a Free Syrian Army commander and his significant other. Since then the commander has been discredited and disappeared from view.

Unknown in the west, Syria has always had a reputation among the countries of the Middle East for a raucous sexual humour, which has its origins in the souk or street life, but was rarely expressed in polite, refined society. I first encountered it while researching the country's racy lingerie culture. Soon I discovered a universe of mobile phone thongs, and panties and bras that played pop songs, vibrated, lit up or fell apart at the clap of a hand. From such revelations emerged my book with Rana Salam, *The Secret Life of Syrian Lingerie: Intimacy and Design*.

The underwear was *shaabi* in nature – populist and vulgar. It was a design culture that succeeded as a home-grown fashion industry and an underground export success story that flourished under dictatorship. Here were products designed and manufactured by religious Muslim families for an observant clientele, which sold as far afield as the malls of Saudi Arabia and the Middle Eastern trinket stores of Shepherd Bush market.

However it is also an industry with sinister undertones, explained Laila. In her view, this lingerie reflected "the habit of a deeply repressive society, but one that was sexually oriented and carried on Scheherazade's *A Thousand and One Nights* traditions. It keeps people absent-minded and later exploits them in a vicious network of tradition, religiosity and authority."

Dirty Jokes

Equally as lurid as the lingerie's grab holes and revealing netting or zippers were the sexual jokes and banter between men and women at parties. The political scientist Ammar Abdulhamid gave me an example, about a ladies' group, which met on a regular basis for coffee each week and chatted about problems they had with their husbands. When a woman in the group looked unaccountably happy, the others asked her, what was going on, and she said: "Yesterday my husband, Abu Ali came in from work. As he changed his clothes, I stuck my hands between his legs and told him, 'Abu Ali, your balls are very cold. Can I warm them up?' *It was a night to remember!*"

The next time the women met, another in their group seemed surprisingly content and her friends quizzed her and she explained,

"When my husband came home from work, he was changing his clothes. I stuck my hands between his legs, saying, 'Abu Antar, your balls are very cold, can I warm them up?' *It was a night to remember!*"

On the third occasion, one woman arrived to the coffee morning with a black eye and walking with a limp, which shocked her friends who cried out, "What happened to you?" "Well," she sighed, "when Abu Muhammad came in from work and changed his clothes, I put my hands on his balls, and said, 'Hey, Abu Muhammad, why are your balls warm, not like the balls of Abu Ali and Abu Antar?' It was a night to remember!"

The joke, vulgar and misogynistic, has a violent twist at the end, like much of Syrian humour. It has echoes in a famous cartoon by the country's premier editorial caricaturist Ali Ferzat. A tortured prisoner hangs in a cell where body parts have been strewn around it. On the floor, his jailer, sitting in front of a TV and watching a soap opera, is sobbing oblivious to his surroundings. Just as Laila suggested, romance and sex are distractions from day to day life under totalitarianism.

Her late father, a prominent political dissident, told her a joke that took place during his years in Palmyra, a notorious jail located near the famous archaeological site in remote south-central Syria. An inmate had been badly tortured by guards, after a mass demonstration by prisoners had gone badly wrong. Once the man, who had been beaten to a pulp, was returned to their hut, everyone surrounded him, feeling terrible – all that is, except for one prisoner who pushed his way to the front, and asked, "Did they curse your mother's vagina (*kiss imak*)?" To which everyone burst into laughter. Nothing else mattered, Laila shrugged and smiled, "Rest assured, he could go to heaven. His and his family's honour were intact."

Of course, the question remains: isn't humour and chatter about sex somehow "too trivial" to indulge in – especially at a time when

according to most recent estimates there are 60,000 Syrians dead, two million displaced inside the country and nearly a million languishing in refugee camps in Jordan, Iraq, Egypt and Turkey? In the current tragedy as much as in broken societies elsewhere down the years, gallows humour is a typical response to political horror. Sex and humour are subversive ways of reaffirming one's humanity in the face of oppression. And satire itself is a sharp weapon – the last thing that the Ba'athist regime seems able to cope with is mockery and derision. After cartoonist Ferzat breached what he called "the barrier of fear" and started making satirical drawings of Bashar Assad, he was attacked by pro-regime thugs in August 2011 who told him, "Bashar's boot is better than you," before breaking his hands. Ferzat, who has since healed, lives in exile in Kuwait and has started drawing again.

Sex and the Single Muslim

The newly translated into English novel *The Silence and the Roar* by Nihad Sirees explores the entwining of humour, sex and violent intimidation that is typically Syrian. Originally published as *Al Samt Wal Sakhab* in 2004, it relates a day in the life of Fathi, a banned writer who survives censorship and threats by laughing and having sex. Sirees, a writer from Aleppo who is better known in the region for his historical television series *The Silk Road*, did not succumb to the feel-good factor that permeated the early years of Bashar Assad's presidency. He had been one of the country's intellectuals who had high hopes for change during the short-lived Damascus Spring of 2000. Once it became too dangerous to speak out and sign petitions, Sirees withdrew, watched and waited. *The Silence and the Roar* was the fruit of his frustrations, and is set against a hysterical daylong mass march with crowds proclaiming their love of the "Great Leader" under the menacing eye of an unnamed country's secret police.

The tense fragmenting of family – the one institution that should provide a safe haven from an intrusive state – lies at the heart of the novel. Fathi's 56-year-old widowed mother who spends her

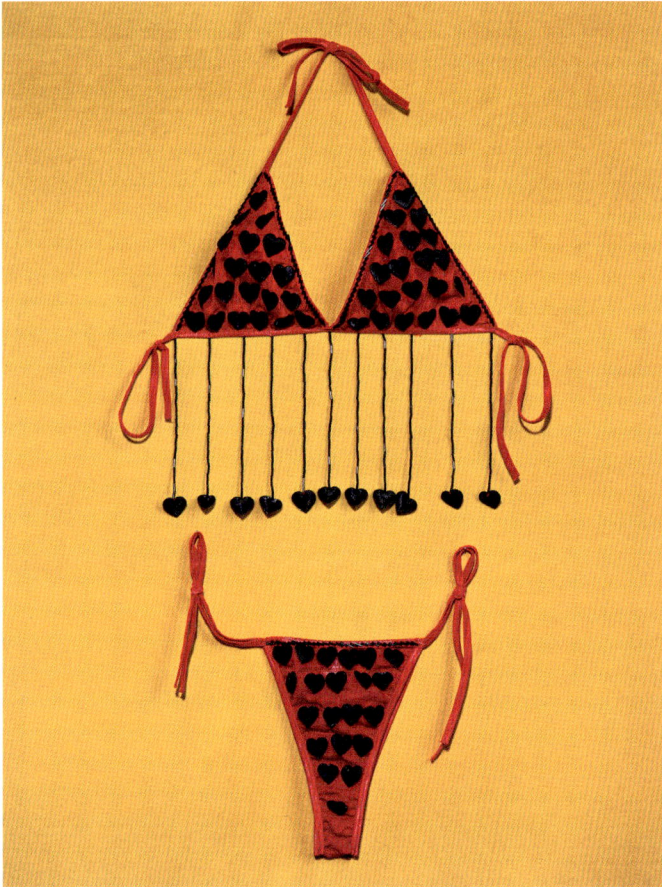

With the levels of violence rising across Syria, it is understandable that people retreat to their bedrooms. Another 28-year-old activist believed there has been a marked sea change towards having sex among the younger generation. As we discussed the waves of children born in the Dheisheh Palestinian refugee camp in the Occupied West Bank – the product of months-long lockdowns and no electricity from Israel in the 1990s – he suddenly cried out, "This is exactly what's happening in Syria today."

However Laila wasn't convinced that a sexual revolution was in full bloom. Too many people, she stressed, have fled the country and some of those who remained at home have gravitated towards what they know – conservatism and religion.

A New Business Model for Islam

Sex and humour are not new in the Arab world. In the eighth century, African-Arab author, raconteur and theologian Al-Jahiz was making penis jokes in Basra. His most famous quip about the Al Quraysh tribe of the Prophet Muhammad would only incense Salafis today. Salwa Gaspard of Saqi Books, in London, observed that even though a sanitised version of *A Thousand and One Nights* was first told to them as children in Beirut, the humour and sexual innuendo of the East's most famous folktales were not completely lost because "they could imagine what was going on". Today, there is a crisis in Arab publishing. The only books published in their thousands and selling in the region's book fairs, where the Arab world's gets its reading material, aren't the classics but religious books on Islam.

time on her bed, watching the march on TV, preens herself for an upcoming marriage to a regime official, who has the writer in his sights. Meanwhile Fathi, disturbed by the roar of the crowd, seeks solace or silence in his girlfriend's bed. In the west, there is a tendency to consider sex as a private, consenting act between individuals. In a country where people are used as pawns by the state, Sirees told me he believed that an active unfettered sex life can be an expression of freedom and a very public stance against repression.

At the beginning of the Syrian revolution in 2011, there was a little known offshoot of the struggle that no one at that time dared to acknowledge publicly. The Syrian artist Khalil Younes, originally from Damascus, called it "shy trials" or experimentation with changing sexual attitudes when we first talked in May last year.

Nine months later, as a fully fledged war engulfed the country, he said more and more young Syrians are revealing their lives in detail: who they are looking for, what they want and how they feel on their Facebook page status updates. It has become a trend among the young because they are encountering so many Muslims just like themselves engaging in candid self-reflection. And this has led to more open attitudes towards sex.

"When the Arabs were confident they talked and wrote a lot about sex. Once their culture declined and the people become less self assured, sex was not discussed in public," revealed Dr Shereen El Feki, UN Commissioner on HIV and the Law. She explores mediaeval Islamic sexual manuals and encyclopaedias in her forthcoming, impressively researched book, *Sex and the Citadel: Intimate Life in a Changing Arab World*. Yet, Abdulhamid, a former religious fundamentalist who later changed his mind about extremism and wrote a novel entitled Menstruation, recalled that sex education was relegated to evening courses at a local mosque, where women's bodies, their fluids and cycles were much discussed and analysed. This and the continuing popularity in the region of Abdelwahab Bouhdiba's *Sexuality in Islam*, first publishing in 1975, surely must counter the prevailing western misconception that Islam is somehow prudish.

On the Syrian street sexual punning was readily displayed in the souk on the lingerie stalls or in the plate glass windows of women's clothing shops in the form of jokey, fun underwear. Eastern European women modelled bits of Lycra and feathers – not in a sexualised manner as seen in the advertising of Victoria Secret or Calvin Klein, but in photos by local photographs that featured nipples, crotches and big friendly smiles.

Now the lingerie companies are not selling the volume they did when Gulf Arabs in niqabs flocked to their wholesale showrooms and factories. Still, during the uprising, trade of lingerie flourishes. As bookseller Stephen J. Gertz in his blog Booktyrst wrote over a year ago, despite the increasing danger in Syria's capital city, it was "revealing that for purveyors of lingerie in Damascus' souk Al Hamidiyah business is good, if not brisk." More recently, a camera during a BBC news report panned along the souk's store and stalls, and captured torso mannequins in colourful lingerie outfits.

The justification that the lingerie served a much-needed purpose – to break the ice – in traditional Muslim marriage, between the sexually inexperienced on their wedding night, will no doubt pacify the Islamist fighters of Al-Nusra Front – if and when they finally reach souk Al Hamidiyah. Not even they will be able to stand in the way of the lingerie proprietors. These stalwart Sunni religious families are exactly the kind of savvy Muslim businessmen whom the Syrian philosopher and academic Sadik Al-Azem maintained will be at the forefront of a moderate and commerce-minded Islam poised to takeover the country once the violence ends.

The Syrians – "the Chinese of the Middle East" – have always found a way to make a profit. Even at the height of the Hafez Assad dictatorship, cotton lingerie manufacturers in Aleppo sold literally tons of ill-fitting underwear and T-shirts, one told me, to the Soviet Union – perhaps the real motivation behind the Russian government's disdain of Syrian aspirations for freedom. Recently a new phrase has been coined for a more tolerant interpretation of Islam borne more directly out of the experience of the countries in the Levant (not Saudi Arabia), which respects citizenship and individual and minority rights while placing a healthy emphasis on business. Its name "Shami Islam" borrows from "Sham," the classical Arabic for Syria, which later came to represent Damascus, a city known for its ancient mercantile past.

The capital's sexy lingerie industry was never considered part of *tanfees*, a popular cultural theory which identified certain movies, TV mini-series, theatre, literature and even Ali Ferzat cartoons as vehicles to vent anti-regime views, thereby releasing the pressure within a heavily controlled Syrian society. Yet, none of these cultural productions ever impeded the imprisonment or torture of political dissidents in Palmyra prison.

Between the political elite – both dissident and pro-regime – on one side and the vibrant and sometimes coarse Arab street, on the other, there has always been an immense disconnect. This gap is due in part to class and education, but also to language. Middle

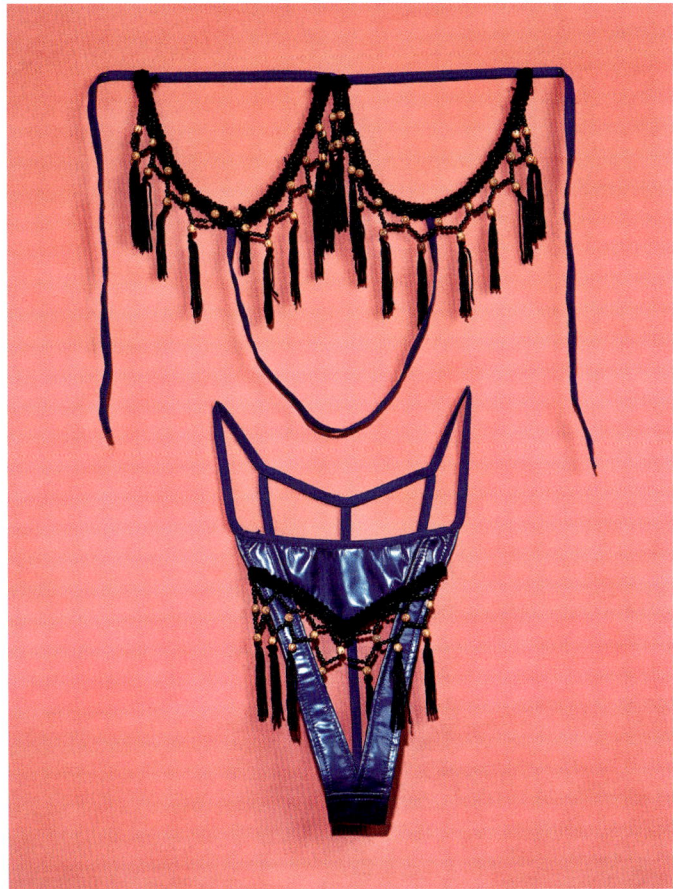

Easterners of substance and distinction were expected to write and express themselves in formal, proper Arabic. The revolution that will probably outlast all of those that began in 2011 is the one presently taking place in communications and social media. Under the pressure of the on-going conflict, young Syrians have adopted a more direct, sometimes crude, language on Facebook to convey their frustrations, hopes and desires. For them, sex and humour have become the *tanfees* of the Syrian uprising.

"No Sex Please, We're Syrian: Confessions from the Lingerie Drawer" was written on the occasion of "Sex and Humour as a Response to Syrian Dictatorship, Violence and Oppression", a panel with Nihad Sirees, Ghalia Kabbani and Malu Halasa, chaired by Rosie Goldsmith and supported by English Pen, at Waterstone's Piccadilly, London, on January 30th, 2013.

Books mentioned in the essay:
• *Sex and the Citadel: Life in a Changing Arab World* by Dr Shereen El Feki (London: Chatto and Windus) 2013 • *The Silence and the Roar* by Nihad Sirees, translated by Max Weiss (London: Pushkin Press) 2013 • *The Secret Life of Syrian Lingerie: Intimacy and Design* by Malu Halasa and Rana Salam (San Francisco: Chronicle) 2008 • *Sexuality in Islam* by Abdelwahab Bouhdiba, translated by Alan Sheridan (London: Saqi Books), 2004 • *Menstruation* by Ammar Abdulhamid (London: Saqi Books) 2001

Stretching Boundaries

BY PHILIP FIMMANO
DESIGN BY BART HESS

The work of Bart Hess is of the most tactile and intuitive nature. He first delved into instinctive textiles when studying at the Design Academy Eindhoven, where he created *A Hunt for High Tech*, a collection of materials that mimicked the bestial outer layers of unfamiliar hybrid species, accompanied by an evocative film that brilliantly brought his concepts to life.

Over the past six years, Hess has developed an impressive roster of work. He has pinned, stretched, slimed and scraped materials in relation to the human body, and collaborated with the likes of Lucy McRae, Nick Knight, Lady Gaga, Iris van Herpen, Walter van Beirendonck and Mugler. In 2013, he was the recipient of the Stichting Profiel prize and his work was the subject of a mid-career survey at the Rijksmuseum Enschede. The exhibition notes explained that Hess creates another world, one "in which technology melds body and object... When we don the materials and applications that Hess has created, we are transformed into a new but completely logical creature."

Hess feels that our bodies are increasingly becoming a platform for sensitive and interactive technology, and has constantly exposed the intimate relationship materials have upon our skin, including a concept for Philips Design that mounted an electronic tattoo underneath the skin's surface. "It felt like a natural instinct for me to start working on the body. When I create a new design I always place it on my own skin even-though it originally was created as, for example, a flooring material. The fascinating thing about it for me is the combination of a skin and a material. By using a material on the body that is not the body's own, but making it look like it could possibly be, I create a tension between the body and material."[1]

Foamy, sweaty, blobular and molecular are the kinds of surfaces that Hess concocts. Flirting with a touch of the grotesque and the macabre, he explains that he tries "to find a balance between beauty and disgust or horror. I think the darker side of beauty has less restrictions because it hasn't been explored that much, which makes it more interesting for me to show to my audience"[2] Through the use of design, film, photography and installation, Hess has found intimate ways for his textiles to communicate with their "audience", and in 2012's Work With Me pop-up studio, he was even able to involve some of them in the making process.

If Hess is on the hunt for tactilities that can transform the design landscape, he is definitely on the right track. By innovating materials that braise, coat or titillate the body, he has opened up a sensual and sexually-charged discourse about the future of smart textiles. Hess introduces materials to our primal needs and innate sense of touch, showing that fabrications will first need to seduce us before they can become part of us.

---

1   Design 360°, interview, 2013

2   idem

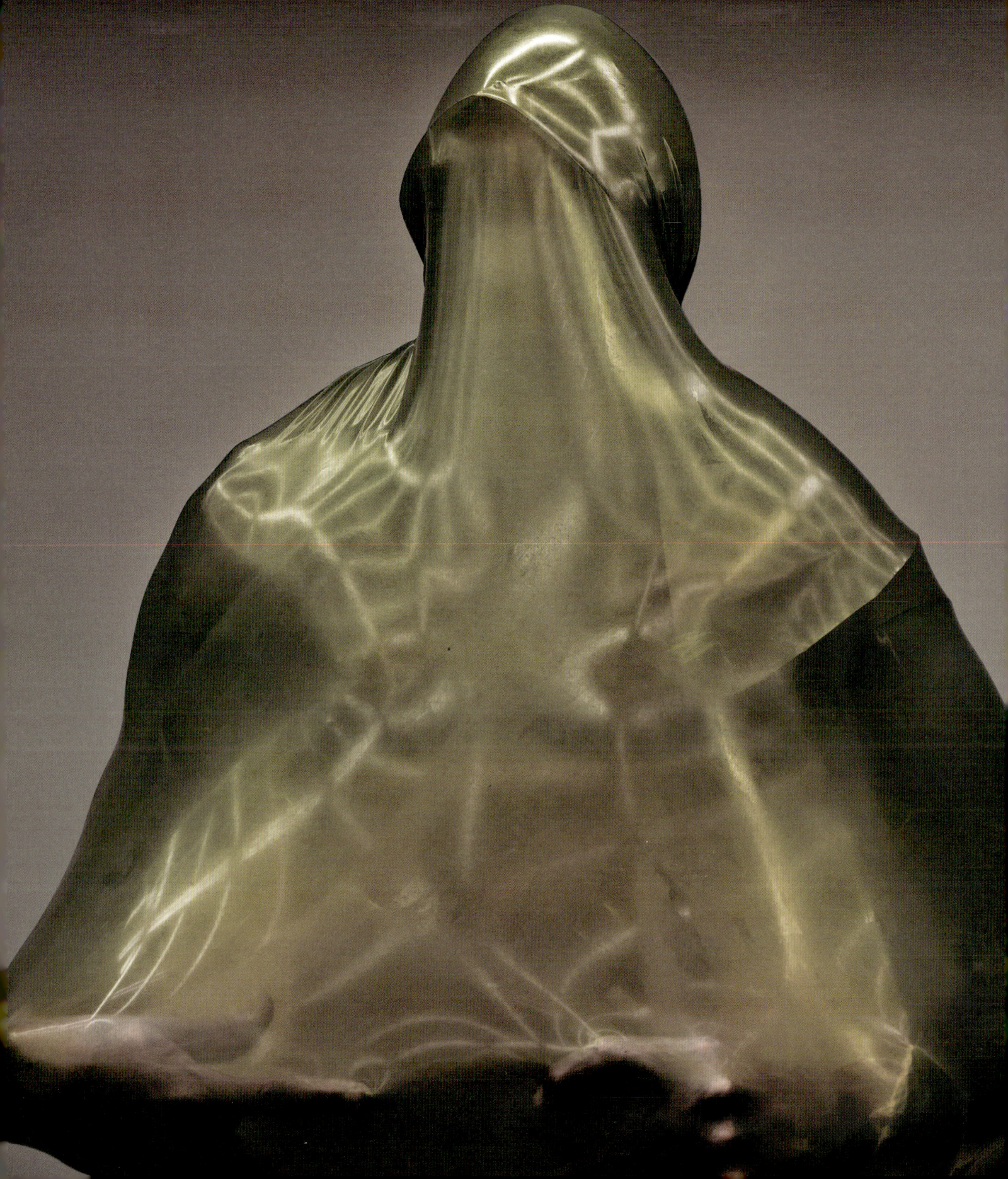

Anymales

PHOTOGRAPHY BY DIDIER ILLOUZ

Since 2006, French photographic artist Didier Illouz has delved into American Indian shamanism and Medicine Cards, divination tools that embrace ancient wisdom to heal and learn from animal semiotics.

Anymales is an experimental series involving the channelling of an animal being by the model which is then incarnated through Illouz's photographic representations and digital retouching. Formulating, deforming, transforming and reforming... The Animistic appropriation of bestial qualities is a revived contemporary current, and Illouz's creatures conjure up hybrid visions that exist somewhere between the world of the spirits and our own.

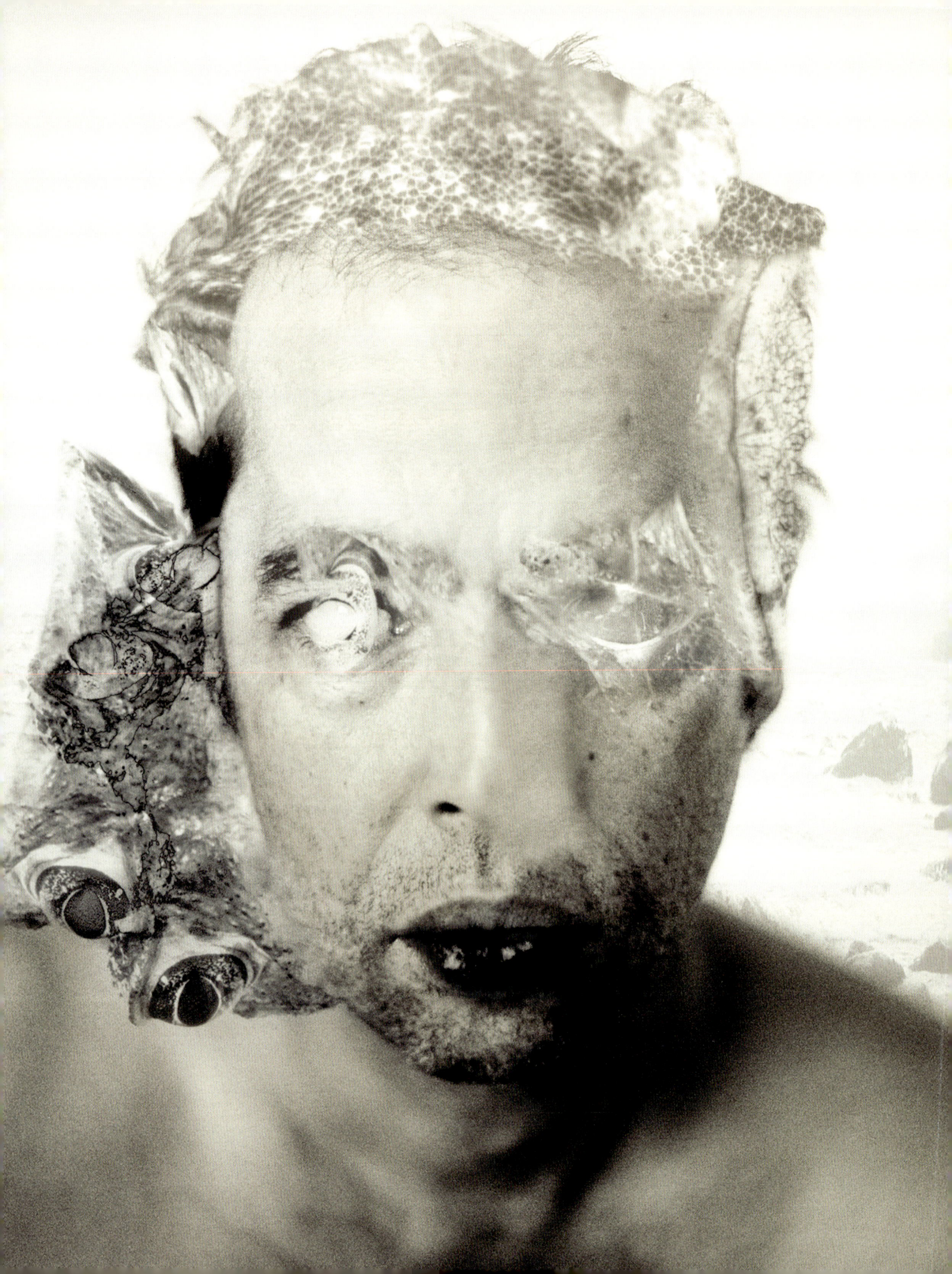

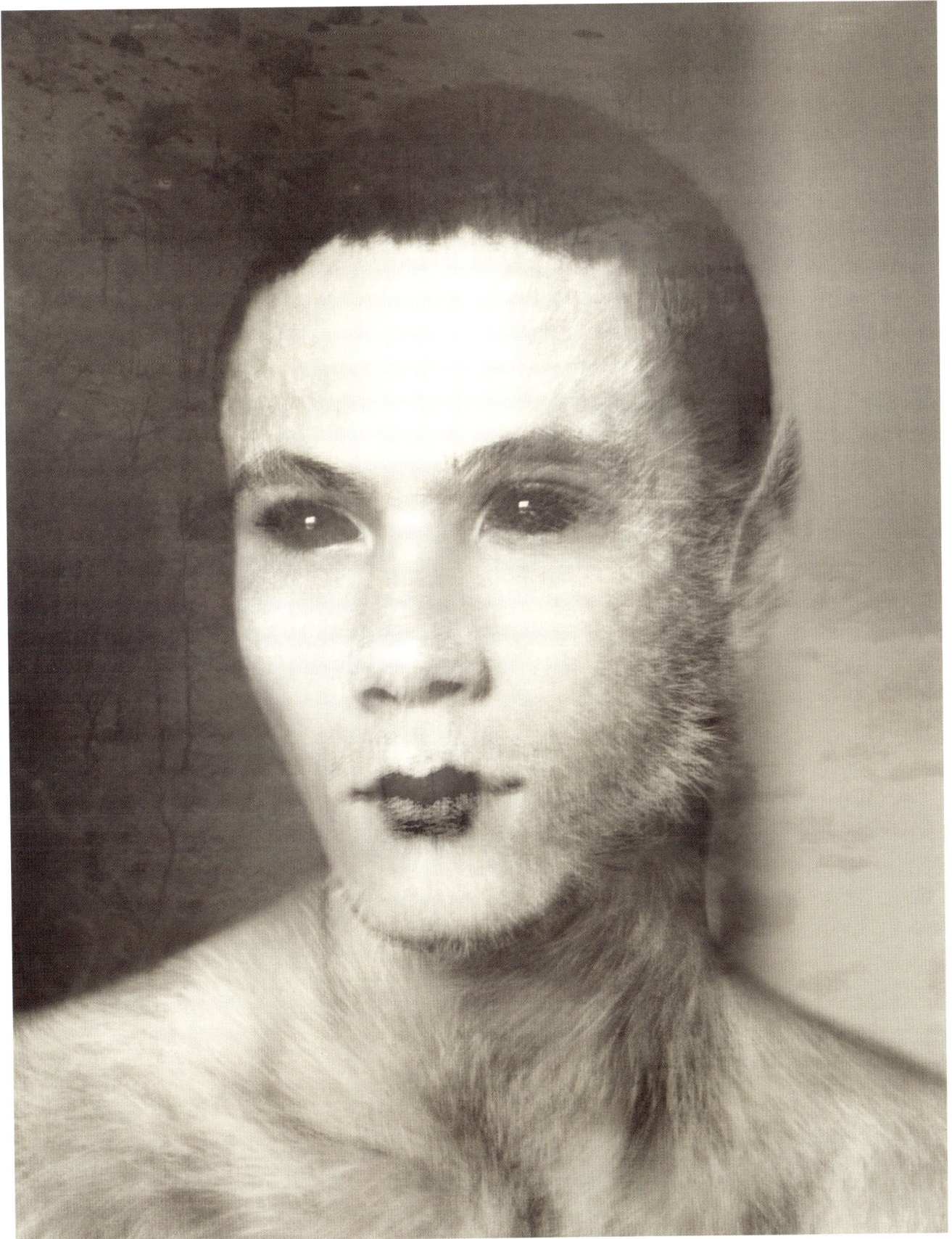

Fascination

INTERVIEW WITH RAVAGE & JOHN SILLEVIS
ILLUSTRATIONS BY ARNOLD VAN GEUNS

What fascinates you about men?
Men who walk by never cease to fascinate us. When sitting on a street terrace, we play our favourite game: giving prizes to the best-dressed ones as they pass by, relying on our sharp eye for men's fashion history.

How do you judge them?
While we often can't agree on the rules of this complex game, we try to focus on a single question: what defines a well-dressed man? "A masterpiece!" is what one used to declare back in the day, when only a small group of men could afford to be dressed well. In the beginning of the 19th century, two interesting archetypes emerged: the Dandy and the Gentleman.

How do you see the Dandy?
To clarify any misunderstandings, a true dandy was someone who dressed with care, without ever being extravagant. Dandies were not boisterous, over-the-top or overstated men, as is often misperceived. It took more to make a dandy; though a pronounced character and insolence surely contributed to what one could call "dandiness". Famous dandies such as Beau Brummel wore a blue riding-coat – since all of Europe was dressed in an English manner at the time – with beige breeches and well-polished boots. It was as simple as that! The only thing for which he needed a lot of time was the tying of the necktie – least we not forget the flourishing necktie of flair! "A well-tied tie is the first serious step in life", as Oscar Wilde once said, and the only weapon a dandy possessed was his power to seduce.

And what about the Gentleman?
The gentleman however – who like the dandy, hardly ever paid his tailor – underlined his status by preferring classic and well-worn clothing that was first worn by his house-staff. "Shabby chic" was therefore already a past phenomenon, also understood by citizens that lived on the other side of the Atlantic, in Boston or at Harvard. But if his swallow-tail didn't arrive back from the tailor on time, this apparently nonchalant gentleman would worry about being forced to appear in a tuxedo at the dinner table, which was considered as "very inappropriately dressed".

What about their details and accessories?
There were hats for every occasion, gloves for both summer and winter, and there were thousands of neckties; of which, three styles were favoured, and silk shawls were considered appropriate for every hour of the day. Fascinated, this man could let his gloved-fingertips slide across the brim of his Borsalino or Homburg. These indispensable accessories are not really part of men's fashions any longer, yet an emerging and interesting trend has appeared in that today's modern men's wardrobe is almost entirely comprised of accessories.

How has dressing up evolved since then?
What has changed since Beau Brummel and the laid-back gentleman is the democratisation of clothing and the evolution of certain codes. While looks such as the "worn-out" and the "aged" are still being used today, sportswear has turned into city wear and has to look brand new. Even the season's must-have hairdo stays impeccable on a football player who after a hard game, still has his hair styled to perfection!

What do you think about style?
Once discrete, the name of a tailor or fashion house is now placed on garments and accessories, branded and able to be recognized at first sight. The dandy – who does still exist – now pays high prices for his clothes and is proud of it; while the gentleman – a dying breed – does the same, but with little result; "it was expensive, but was it worth it?" Once, the aristocracy and the rich set style examples for the rest of society, while today style is mostly inspired by penniless young men from the streets.

What does this mean for fashion in the future?
We see that some old-fashioned attitudes that once defined a

MENSWEAR FETISH

with a totally worn-out aspect. The military uniform fascinates us again too; in the 1970s it was worn to protest against war, nowadays its virile appearance is underlined and with the conviction of his body, man can play a dangerous game of seduction. We're not far removed from the dashing Russian officer in his ultra tight jacket, for whom Anna Karenina left husband and child.

What makes the 21st century special?
We have once again entered a Romantic period. Events around the world point towards change, from the revolutions in the Arab world to the Occupy Wall Street movement that is challenging the capitalistic system we trusted in for so long. Questions about the "I" are being reassessed: what is the place of the individual at a time when technology seems to have the answers to everything?

How does this effect men?
A deeply-rooted emotional feeling is felt in the modern male identity, imaginatively updated as an archetype that was once dressed with a velvet vest, shoulder-length hair and sensitive tears. Confronted with violence, he goes on a poetic and passionate crusade, but also interests himself in folklore fashion and regional traditions; and above all, in nature and our humble place in the world. Heine, Schiller and Byron are each important inspirational references.

Any last thoughts?
Let us throw away the idea of the well-dressed man in order to adopt and admire all these different freedoms with a fascinated eye. The media has a primordial place in culture today, and so we can remember Oscar Wilde's belief that all men are attractive once they have been spoken of.

well-dressed man no longer function. Much has changed; for example, Truman Capote's 1970s view that "There's something really the matter with most people who wear tattoos" has been freed by a generation of often sensitive tattooed men; it seems that nowadays 90 per cent of the world's male population wants to look like a "bad guy."

Are our times as inspiring as in the past?
All in all, we live in fascinating times. We listen to music of different genres, and more books have been published after the Second World War than all the books printed since Gutenberg's invention of the press. Each generation rediscovers and spontaneously adopts the fashions and trends that previous generations have passed on.

Does this mean that anything goes?
While all is fair in fashion, defined codes don't leave much room for improvisation; each style has its own strict rules and rituals. Keeping an eye on detail, long-forgotten tailoring details are now reinterpreted in new outfits. Restyled with precision, silhouettes are reconstructed. This reinvented man is just as easily drawn back into hippy ideals that are revived and used in carefree garments, giving the impression as if we are on our way to a truly better world.

How about technology?
If it is not the history that inspires modern man, then it is the fascinating modern materials that can produce synthetic skin-like tactilities; a second skin, either boyish or in devilish black, also reinterpreted.

Are fashion trends linear?
Opposing extremes sometimes bring us minimalism through architecture and design as inspirational sources, which are then counterbalanced by an opulent trend, possibly inspired by a heavily made-up Venetian Casanova; again, his thick baroque brocade

FETISHISM IN FASHION

111

Designs on Desire

BY PHILIP FIMMANO
PHOTOGRAPHY BY PHILIPPE MUNDA

The organic formations of the natural world evoke irrevocably sensual shapes and naughty notions in the mischievous eye of the beholder. This opens us up to an entirely new vision of nature that can inspire ritualistic relationships with natural materials.

The voluptuous curves of a chubby nude, the rounded cleft of a female sex, the intricacies of pubic curls or the robustness of a sturdy phallus easily make their way into the psyche in the presence of such forms as an uncanny *coco fesse*, a spawning tulip bulb, the deep pearly concavity of a sea shell, or a large and enticing column of smooth driftwood.

ORGANIC FETISH

As happened with historical curiosities, contemporary objects will be inspired by these designs on desire, mimicking nature's innocent erotic forays and translating them into aesthetic incarnations; most notably started by Tom Dixon's innovative dildo, this story is to be followed while technology continues to embrace an organic future.

Perhaps man's favourite stones will become pets to have and to hold at night. The modern Chipko movement of tree hugging rings true at a romantic time when we are in search of connecting to nature and can experience the physicality of bark and trunk in an emotional and erotic way. Some Hindu traditions even procure marriages to a tree, which could inspire a new fetish to cherish forever and ever until death do you part.

ORGANIC FETISH

In the most intriguing of examples, one woman has been known to tie herself naked to a bolder on stormy nights, so overcome by the power of nature's thrusts that she is able to climax through thunder bolts. With the recent influential shockwaves sent out by Björk's *Biophilia* experimentations with Tesla coils, music and culture at large are surely in store for a more intimate symbiosis with Mother Earth.

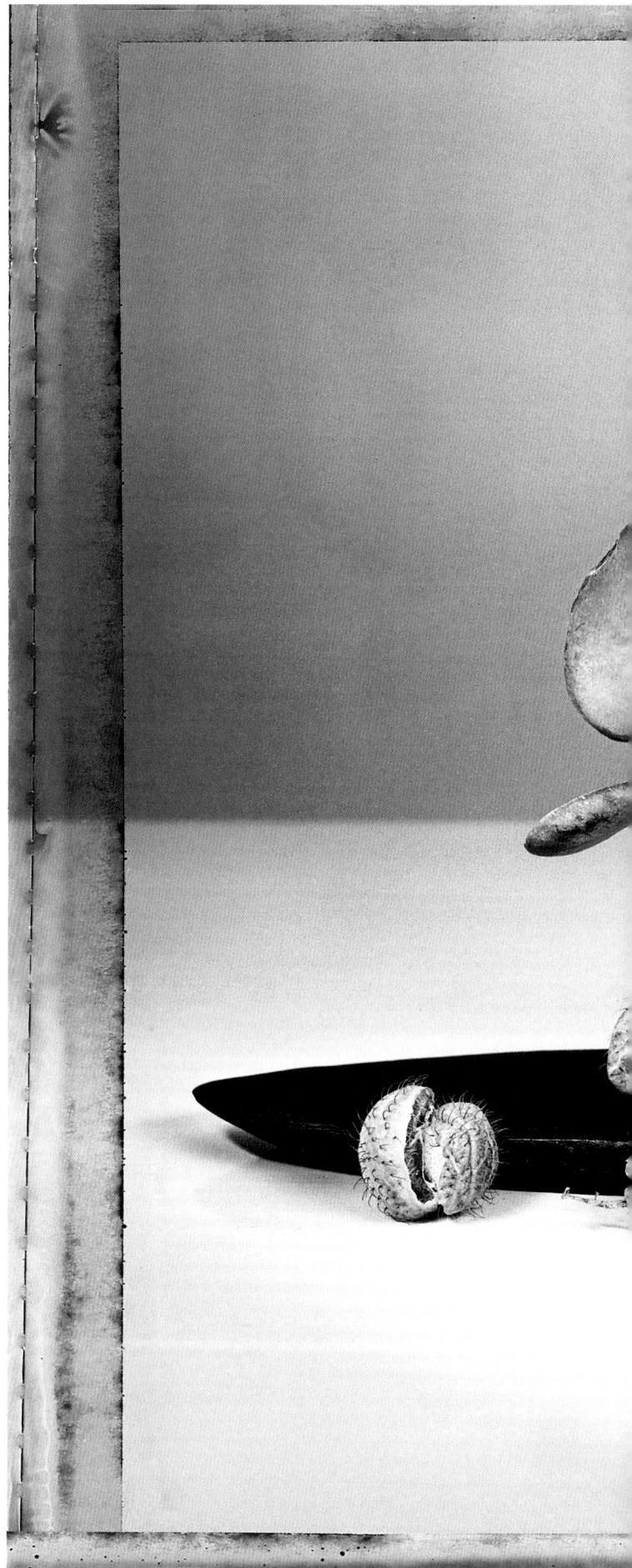

Basic Instinct

PHOTOGRAPHY BY CARSTEN WITTE

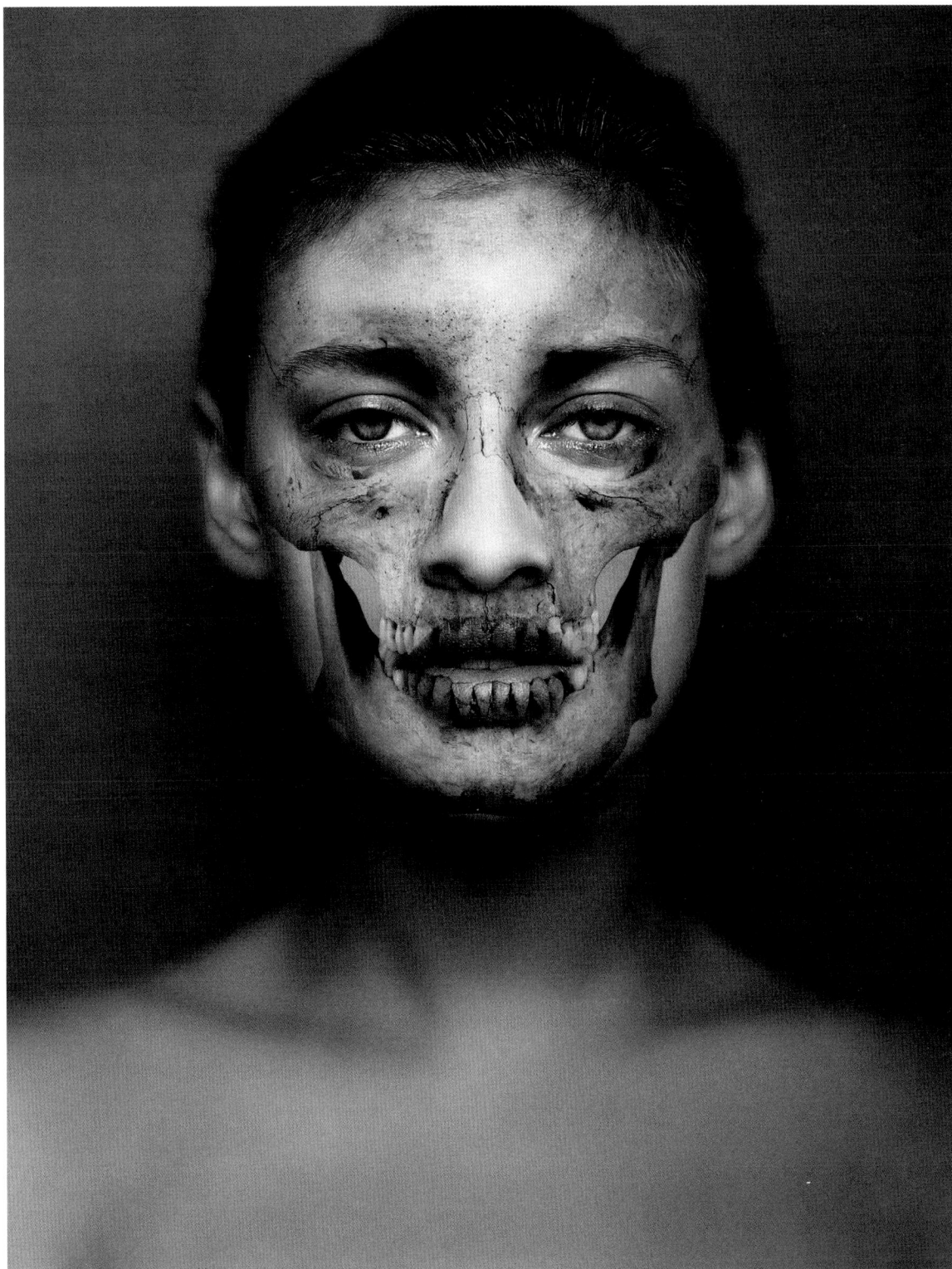

FACE FETISH

Throughout his career, German photographer Carsten Witte has mastered light and shadow in order to reveal the erotic allure of the female body. He has a particular penchant for the face – our windows to the soul – saying "It's always faces that fascinate me (most) and this mysterious purity of really beautiful people".

FACE FETISH

Witte's fascination began in childhood, when he recalls gazing at passers by while walking hand-in-hand with his mother. Focusing on art photography since 1999, he is on a continual quest to extract the essence of his subjects: "Form, colour and transience are reduced to a common denominator". By stripping away superficial layers and any inhibitions, Witte's portraits possess confidence, wild instinct and directness. Yet, their ambiguity is their most powerful asset, and the audience is left wondering where exactly do Witte's creatures come from?

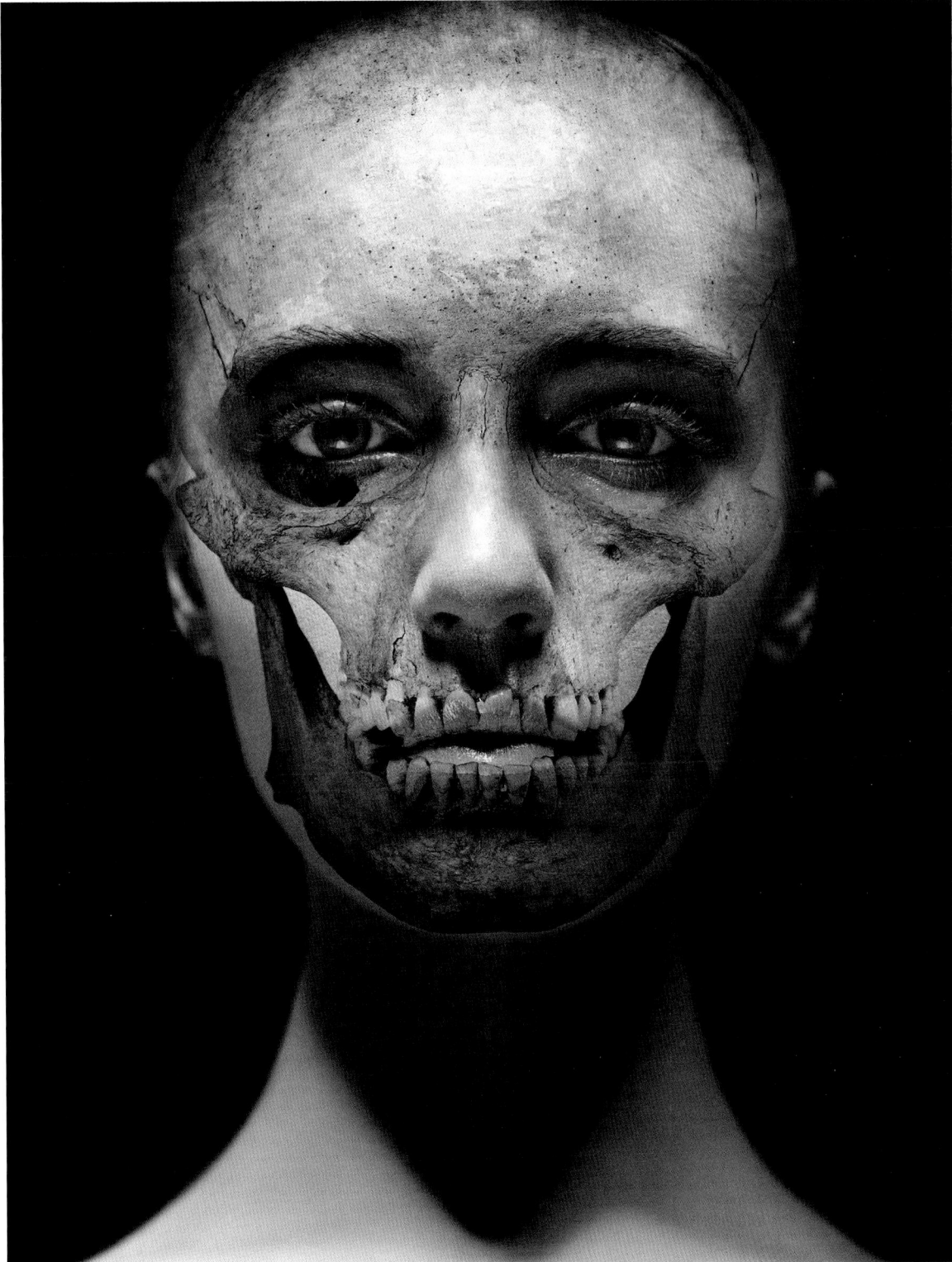

Symbolic Scale

PHOTOGRAPHY BY LON VAN KEULEN

FISH FETISH

Symbols of divine energies held captive in an object, fetishes owe their magical virtues to the natural and spiritual forces that inhabit them. Indeed, fetishes made from plant or animal matter confer upon those who possess them the strengths and virtues of the living organism they represent. As symbols of water, fish are not only quicksilver fast and breathtakingly beautiful, but they are also represented in many cultures tied to fertility, prosperity and good fortune.

It is thus auspicious to take inspiration from our aquatic kin: their bright and sombre colours, their smooth scales, their vivid and subtle patterns, and their iridescent transparencies that can all guide us to swim in new material directions. Technology has much to learn from the organic surfaces and structures of fish, while our desire to dress and live in luminous, shiny matter certainly borders on the fetishistic.

From hardware to soft wear, we will see schools of sustainable fish skins make their ways through our wardrobes, in both synthetics and naturals: sharkskin for sleek suiting, metallic mesh, fin-like transparencies, slippery coatings, ichthyic weaves, printed scales, spots and stripes, fishbone raffias, salmon leathers, metallic yarns and shimmering silks. We can suggest scales even further through glossy layers of sequins or gleaming beads. And the curvaceous mermaid dresses that have flooded the Red Carpet in recent seasons indicate that this fish-tale is only just getting started...

The Complexion of Culture

BY LIDEWIJ EDELKOORT
PHOTOGRAPHY BY MARCEL VAN DER VLUGT

History repeats itself, not always exactly in the same way, but nevertheless inspired by former events and culture. We live a moment of citation, sampling bits and pieces from the tremendous creative energy of our last centuries to again repeat them; blending and reinterpreting, sometimes feeling hopelessly caged by the superiority of things past.

It is (often) simple to forecast the new by knowing that ideas will take their roots in former periods; such as sports clothes becoming fashion, workers' gear taking to the catwalk, garden outfits replaying Bloomsbury, and pyjamas translating our need for extravagance and intimacy at the same time.

It is therefore exciting to occasionally hit a truly original idea born out of our own day and age, which is only just contemporary. One of these moments has been my discovery of our own skin as a cultural icon of epidermic elegance, spawning a plenitude of inspiration for design and a lifestyle to affect our existence far beyond the confines of our glossy media pages. It was a vintage postcard featuring a redheaded woman clothed in a T-shirt of tattoo patterns as far back as 1987 that triggered my imagination and gave way to a whole set of new ideas; muscled matter, coated technology, tattooed textiles, scarification patterns, and above all, a colourcard made of the shades of our human skin for spring/summer 1989. Skin has proven time and time again that it is a long-term social current, full of renewed relevance and an iconic approach to tactility and colour, and the first arrival of flesh-type products, such as stretch textiles, glass fibre and washed silk fabrics, seemed to be an ideogram of an era.

In the late 1980s, Azzedine Alaïa started his skin-tight dresses and a latex blouson, Jean Paul Gaultier designed his tattoo tulle T-shirts and Issey Miyake created bodysuits with primitive body-paint patterns. Yet this first wave didn't take on and fashion had to wait to see it re-emerge stronger and more confident...

The skin movement has simultaneously become political and racial, artistic and aesthetic, hermetic yet tactile; inspired by a generation of artists concerned with the possibilities of cloning, tracing DNA, cosmetic surgery, and the transformation of gender; as explored in a key publication discussing the aesthetic, generic and clinical mutation of the body, documenting the touring *Post-Human* show curated by Jeffrey Deitch in 1992.

Artists working through the 1990s such as Dinos and Jake Chapman, Thomas Grünfeld, Carston Höller and Rosemarie Trockel, among others, depicted this unease and fascination with the possibilities of the human body transcending its corporeal border, while the glass sperm of Kiki Smith and the body fluids of Andres Serrano went under the skin and inside the body. French-born artist Orlan took it all a step further by surgically-enhancing these ideas into the confines of her own body – as did the runway models of Walter van Beirendonck's fashion shows. Jenny Saville's expansive nudes approached the sculptural qualities of the body with such power that her nudes became the most symbolic icons of this movement. Later, her *Closed Contact* photographic collaborations with Glen Luchford explored the painful extremes to which flesh and obsession can be physically and psychologically pushed.

Its way to transmit organic, erotic and signaletic messages to the inner-self makes skin one of the most utilitarian parts of the body and without it to protect us we wouldn't survive in a world full of pollution, climatic change and bacterial scares. It is both fragile and resistant, easily bruised and quickly recovered – the largest organ of our species, *membrana* is rich in function; containing and protecting, nourishing and healing, warming and cooling, exciting and soothing.

Colour has moulded with new materials using manmade fibres and technological finds to give fabrics seemingly human qualities such as breathing, shielding and rejuvenation, empowering design with humanistic shape and intimacy. Like the flesh tones that were once catalogued like paint chips by the Korean artist Byron Kim, all the possible shades of human skin have been transformed into a range of colors: from milky white to the ebony hue, in passing by pale yellows, voluptuous powdery pinks and timeworn reds. The thrill of goose-bumps, the embarrassment of blushing, the relief of sweating and the pampering of skin, are all metaphors for the design of surfaces and the invention of new textile technologies.

Furthermore, body textures influence our materials: the elasticity of skin inspires fibrous fabrics; the velvety, satiny or coarse grains of the epidermis become wovens; the elasticity of the flesh invites muscular materials; the skin's emotional reactivity inspires novel sensorial cloths. Even the skin's blemishes ennoble

textiles, with blushes, freckles and beauty marks becoming seductive elements, while tattooed skins influence patterns and
the transparency of skin generates sensual and vaporous voiles.
Far from inspiring mere garments, skin evokes a new "second
skin" wardrobe.

Man's own colour is sampled to enable us to feel totally nude under increasingly transparent garments, illuminating this feeling
in other industries. Swatch's SKIN collection wraps the world's
thinnest watches around thousands of wrists each day, while a
blender can be gifted with almost mortal shape and tone, and
headphones envelop our ears in organic and soft skin matter.
Animal hides are transformed from natural darks to cross-dress
as human fashions and create naked shoes, bare handbags and
nude jackets. We are hungry for tactile sensations and when
coupled with lipstick red, these skin tone leathers even make for
quite erotic car interiors. This insatiable thirst for tactility means
that consumers' choices have become determined by touch as
much as vision; in a direct reaction to virtual reality, and as an
affirmation of the materiality of things to come. Today, young
students manifest a continuing interest in skin metaphors; they
map global colour in paints, produce skin-inspired textiles, design body-built furniture and write scenarios for the skin-driven
spas of the future.

Architecturally, the idea of the second shell of a building con-
tinually manifests itself, from the use of paper and cut steel by
ARO in New York to the fiberglass transparencies inherent in
Shigeru Ban's *Naked House*. In our domestic interiors, we witness
skin's influence on a daily basis: the opaque packaging of an Eau
d'Issey after-shave bottle, the matte resins of a Dinosaur Design
vase or the spongy sensuality of a clenched Mogu teddy bear.
Even some flowers are engineered to look like us nude.

In design, Hella Jongerius designed the ultimate tactile *Pushed
Washtub* (1996) and Jurgen Bey connected opposites by assem-
bling and covering different period chairs with a new PVC coat-
ing in *Kokon* chairs (1995). These now historic references made
for a bare, blended and sometimes blind design; void of detail,
dependent on volume and touch alone.

Such silent experiences have led us to our new century with our
eyes closed into a naked world of padded sound, veiled furniture and coated technology. Future textile systems have been
conceived through experimental projects like ElectroTextiles'
soft hardware for IDEO: *Fabrications* is a range that includes a
keyboard, telephone and remote control made of ElekTex, the
world's first viable fabric structure that can sense the location
and pressure of human touch – a highly innovative fabric that
follows the function of our own skin.

Every year, fashion magazines reinvent this nudism, still herald-
ing it as a newly-born idea, inviting us to further explore our
own body for inspiration; not just our own skin but also our
sentiments, evolution and the very matter from which we are
comprised: flesh, bone, water, minerals, hair and skin. Emotions
play a key role in the understanding of these internal discover-
ies, bringing us closer to our cognitive and sensorial dimensions
while we grow further into the future. I believe that the interest
we witness in ourselves as a unique and inspirational source is a
healing process that will continue to bring new visions and surprising vibrancy to both art and design – just like skin, flexible
and resilient.

Today, skin is making yet another appearance in a burlesque and
provocative way. The skin colours are translated into nude corsets and skin-tone bodysuits that are related to clinical details,
inspired by prostheses and body parts. A fetishistic approach
that demonstrates the victim as a fashion icon. All dressed up
with masks and veils, ready to go on stage for the catwalk of the
future.

Tomorrow, man no longer will need the anecdote and the narrative to express himself in illustrative fashions, but will move
towards a more abstract and sculptural approach to form, including that which our being is made of. Our skins' curing properties
promise a new era of biotechnical creation in which designers
will one day grow shape and texture, the DNA-design of the future. National Geographic once published a cover story called
"Unmasking Skin", outlining that no artificial simulation known
to man can truly capture the complexity of the body's prime
component, the one that keeps us in touch with the world. I, on
the other hand, believe that design will keep on trying.

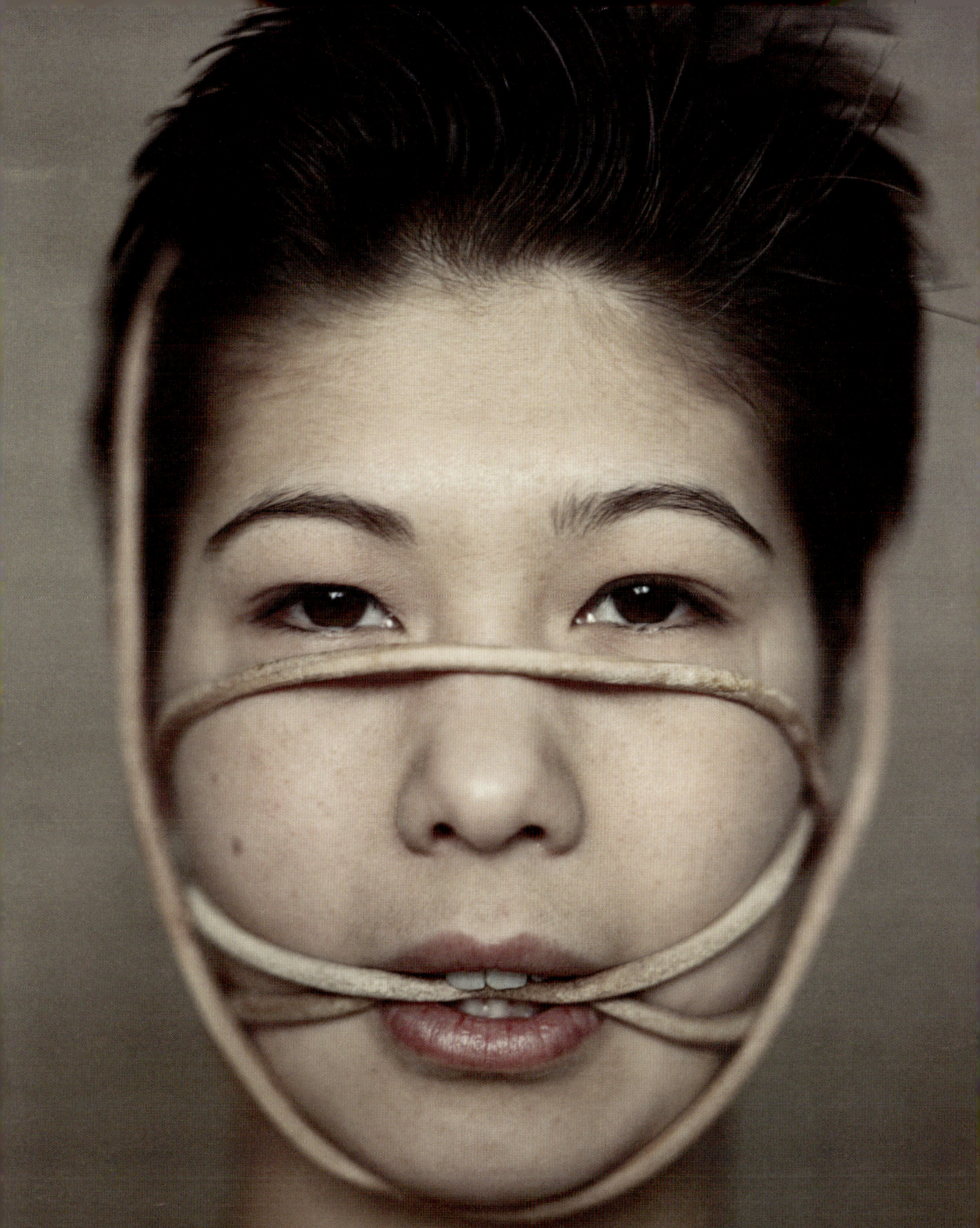

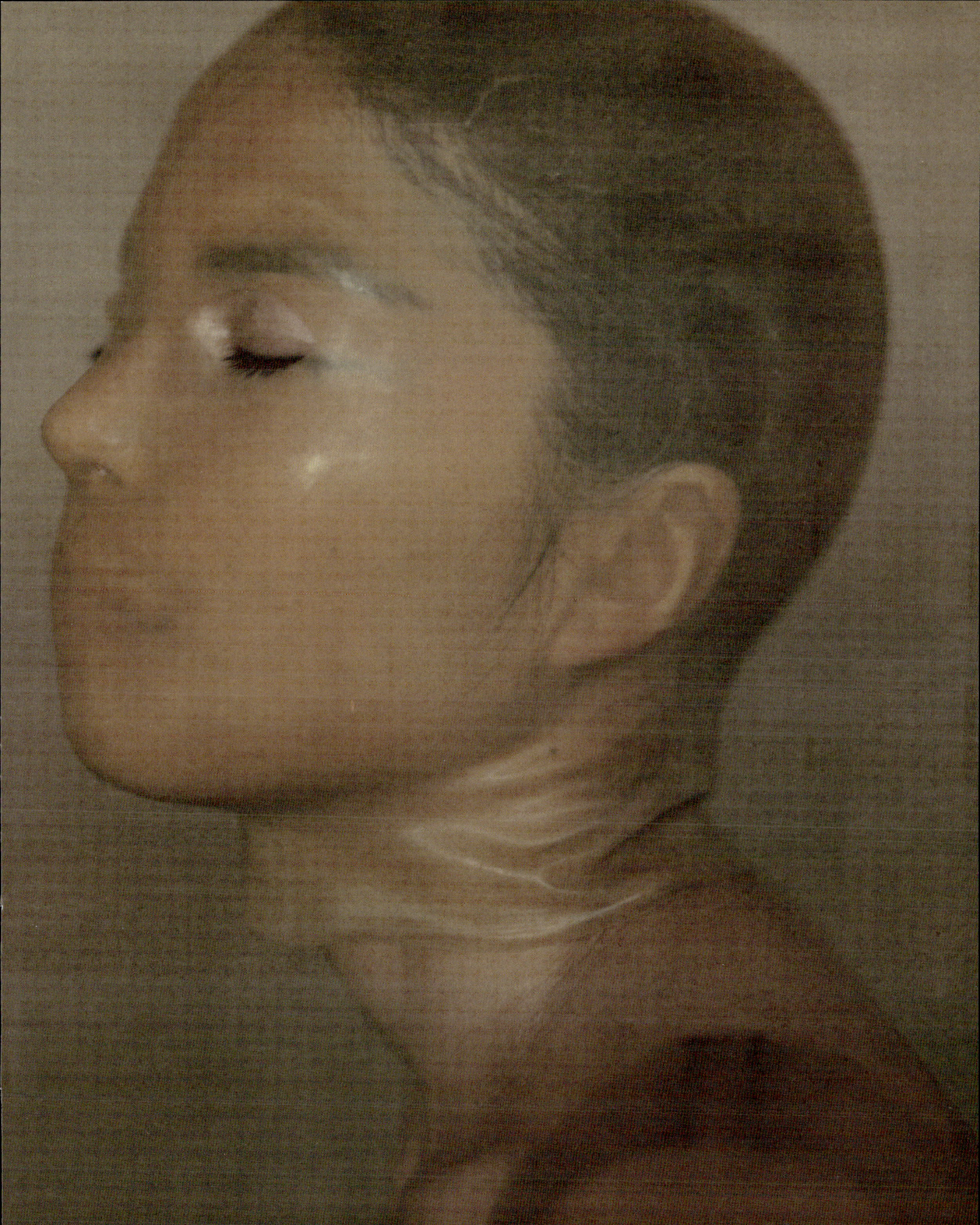

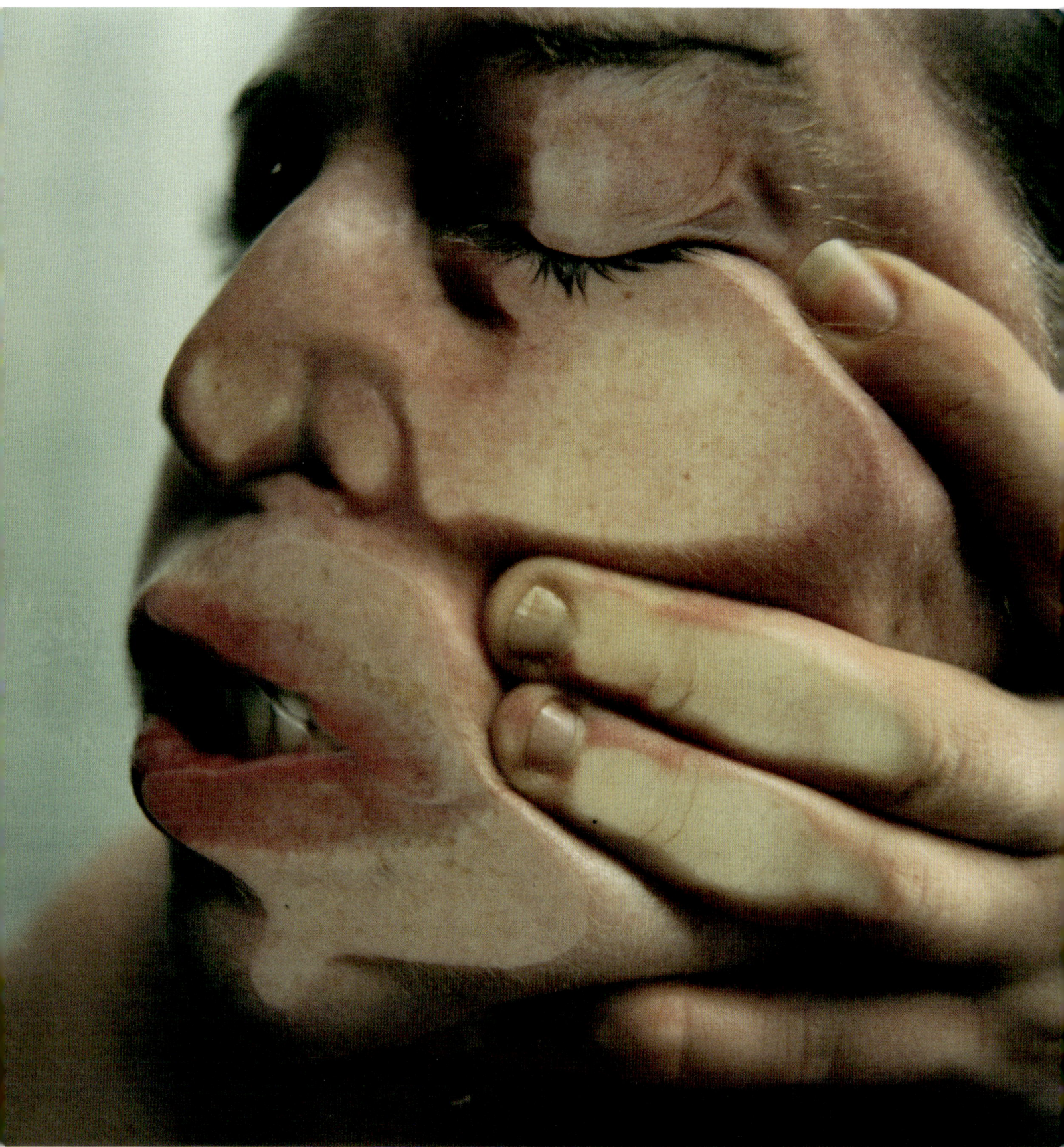

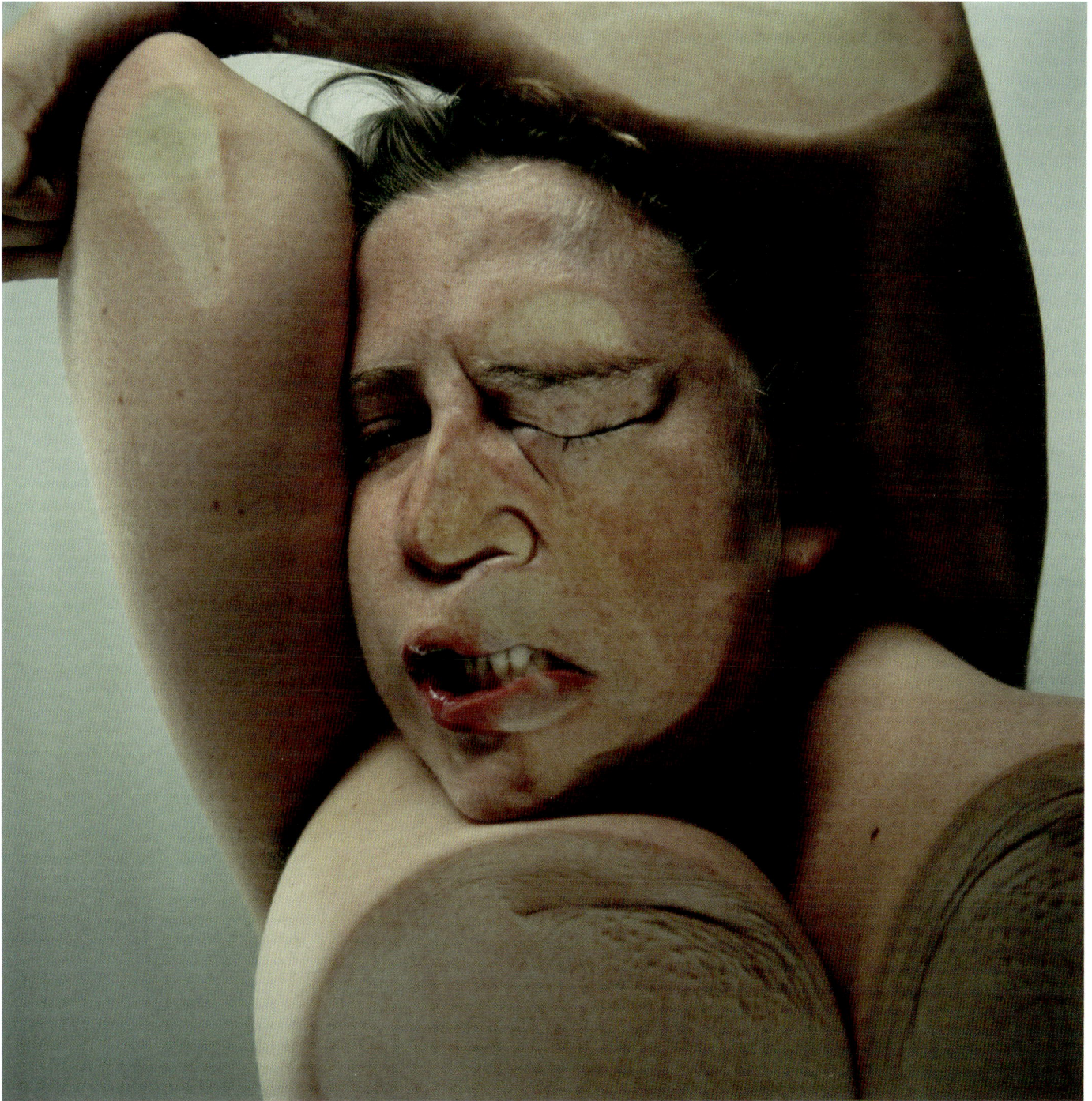

Closed Contact

BY JENNY SAVILLE
IN COLLABORATION WITH GLEN LUCHFORD

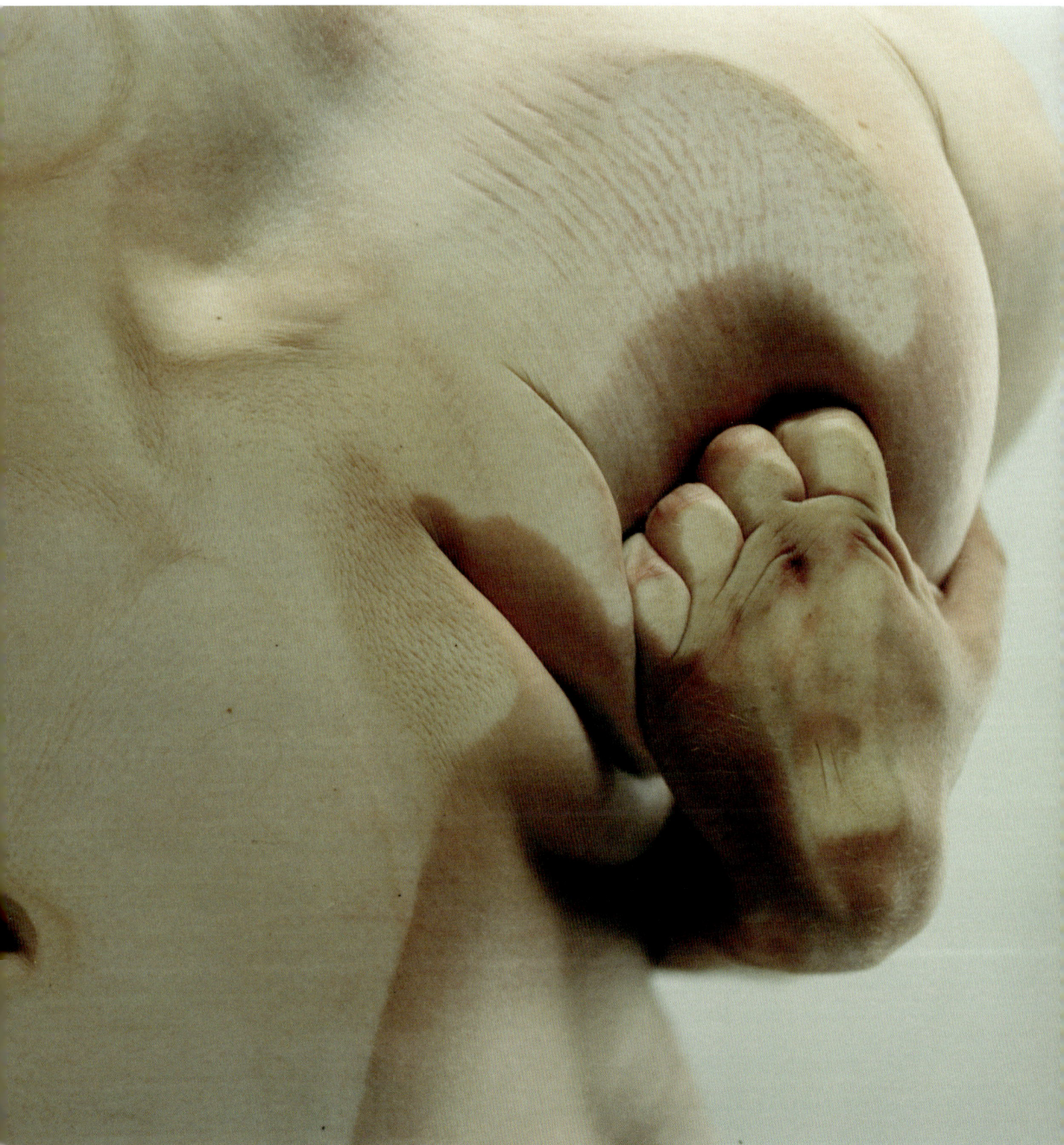

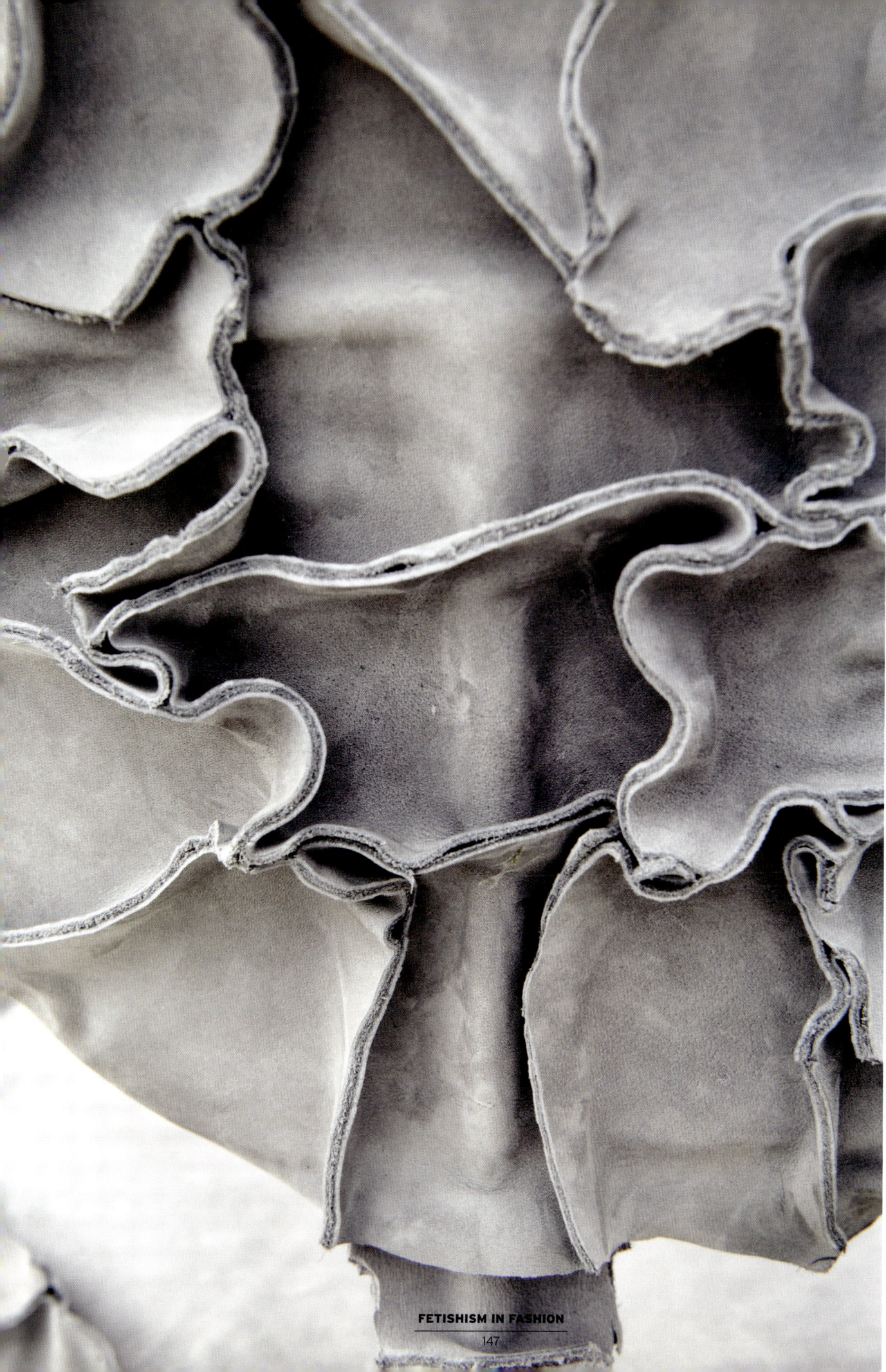

The Found and the Fragment

BY SUSANNAH HANDLEY
DESIGN BY PEPE HEYKOOP

The *Skin Collection* by Studio Pepe Heykoop is a must-have for all fragment fetishists. Scraps of trashed, unsalable leather are formed over the skeletons of junked street-abandoned or second-hand furniture to create award-winning designs. It's a case of Frankenstein gone right. The fleshiness of leather has long made the material a favourite in the fetishist's wardrobe but a lingering aura of sensuality haunts the material, however innocently it is camouflaged. Ingeniously jig-sawed together, skin oddments take on the character of ill-defined body parts viewed through a peephole. Creases, folds, textures, skin tones, inviting touch, vaguely erotic but somehow simultaneously wholesome. Eroticism, of course, lives in the eye of the beholder and the motivations behind the designs of Studio Pepe Heykoop, we have to respectfully acknowledge, are driven by much more ideologically ethical impulses.

Pepe Heykoop is a contemporary Dutch designer of both furniture and objects living in Amsterdam. His principled disposition towards design was nurtured during his studies at the renowned Design Academy in Eindhoven, graduating in 2008. His *A Restless Chairacter* rubber bendable chair which disconcertingly wobbled as if alive itself, won first prize at the 2009 imm D^3 contest in Cologne. In the same year, he joined the Dutch Invertuals collective, a dynamic group of former Design Academy graduates.

With a mission to embrace waste and re-make ready-mades he has transformed mass-manufactured outcasts, underfoot debris and material orphans of failed quality control into one-off, hand-crafted prize exhibits. The furniture industry alone rejects 25 to 30 per cent of skins, those that are scratched, scarred, faded or imperfectly dyed. Studio Pepe Heykoop works with anything from discarded hard wood off-cuts to children's' toy bricks, lambskin patchwork or recycled pewter.

Scandalous squandering is an everyday story in the materials world where it is considered better business to burn or dispose of products rather than donate them. It's hard to find an idealist in a boardroom. Heykoop is perhaps idealistic but he is surely not a dreamer. Recently he has set up a studio foundation in the red light district of Mumbai. Originally established by his cousin, the Tiny Miracles Foundation gives work and training to impoverished women and provides an education programme for young girls. His "ultimate goal is to pull this 700-person community out of poverty by providing healthcare, education and jobs within eight years". Here in the slums, are made the leather lampshades and candelabras that were shown during the 2013 Salone del Mobile. Heykoop has a talent for making unpredictable combinations: who would have thought of bringing the slums of Mumbai to Milan?

Perception stimulates desire and Pepe Heykoop can magic desirable objects from dustbin salvage. As he puts it himself, a chair lying in the street is invisible but when it is rescued and re-designed, it sits in a gallery window, admired as an art object.

Emotional Pornography

BY PHILIP FIMMANO
CREATIONS BY AOI KOTSUHIROI

I kept these dead birds on my shoulder, my body was a branch. I saw death as a pile of sand, a dialogue of dust. Around my mouth I kept these dusts from you, I looked down at my legs covered with white and it seemed to me that all this nudity was harmless. I was suspended to nothing, I lived in that hallway, sitting on this waiting chair, its body and mine discussed, I touched its scars let by pain and distress, they refused to yield, still healing like a new skin which grows after a winter of sleep.

And so we enter the dark world of Aoi Kotsuhiroi, a place of mystery and magic where extraordinary objects are crafted. This maker of intriguing things has recently developed a cult following in the fashion world and been included in exhibitions at New York's Museum at F.I.T. and the Arts Décoratifs in Paris. Working entirely by hand, the processes and ingredients employed by the artist read more like an ancient recipe of ingredients concocted by an enlightened elder.

As a self-described "emotional pornographer" who makes shamanic objects, Kotsuhiroi joins cherry-tree wood to solid horn before it is lacquered in fifteen layers of black sap and bound together by animal glues. Leathers are purveyed from kangaroo, bison, and antique elephant pelts, tied up with horsehair and human hair, as well as straps and cord-like trimmings. Time is measured in lunar cycles, and colours are sampled from shadows. Antique Roman gold and glass are selected alongside Carnelian Mala prayer beads and crow feathers.

Kotsuhiroi's objects for the mouth, foot and body are each unique pieces, given poetic titles that come from the literary landscape that she offers. Ideas come to her from "dream autopsies" inspired by intensified moments such as the coolness of the evening, the regret of the moon and the morning fog.[1]

Distinct images are conjured up by memories of these visions and then embedded into the auras of the designs, such as when 'I was double up with seams, and my leg became tattooed with a sky of birds.' Often, a sexual and fetishistic undercurrent both bewilders and empowers the artist, who seems to singlehandedly merge the forlorn sorrow of Romanticism with the Animistic instincts of pre-history:

I stroked my lips swollen with pain, the night opened like a wound, I had to leave. Everything collapsed in that chaos, the noise of the storm became an animal screaming its anger. I had lost teeth in the gravels, I was looking for them and found a dream tooth. I put gloves and I sewed a stone on my sex. It was a stone of sex, a stone to grow roots, I had to tie it well, to sew it well so it can grow on me.

The photographs that Kotsuhiroi takes add another layer to her story; "I think about the void, about muscles in tension, about attachments that work like fluids and circulations, an underground anatomy." Kotsuhiroi's unique fetishes exist "in the margins of the boundaries", where she observes "the invisible, this kind of transition wall between order and disorder".[2]

---

1   Faint Magazine, interview with Tully Walter, March 2012
2   Interview with Le Paradox, July 2012

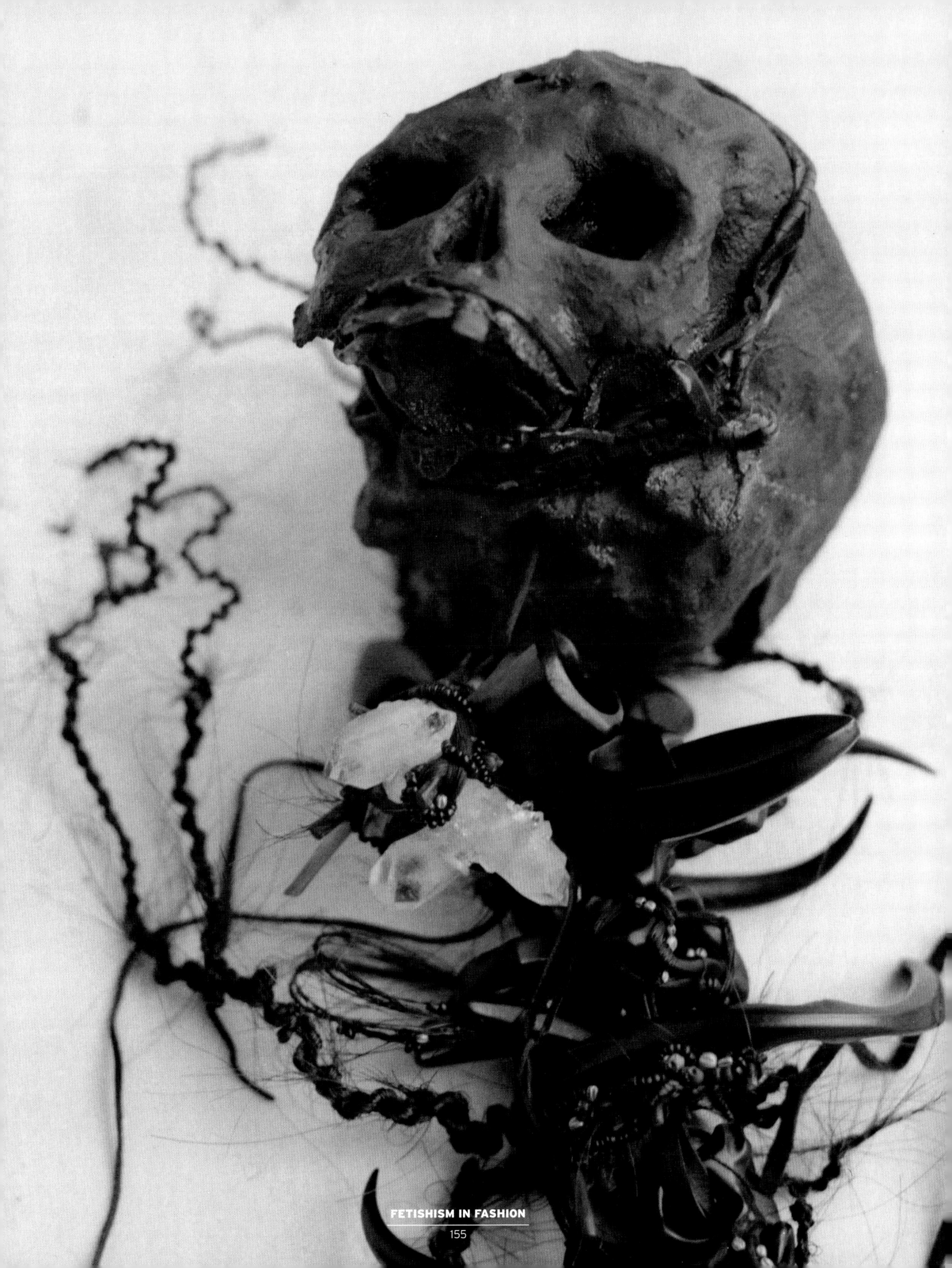

The Monkey In Us

BY ANDREA BRANZI
PHOTOGRAPHY BY PIETER HUGO

There is an important difference between neo-primitivism and the primitive condition. The first can be defined as a cultural movement very close to (or coinciding with) neo-brutalism, marked by the use of unprocessed materials and elements of natural or animal origin. It is the sign of a rejection of the self-referentiality of contemporary design and its hedonistic and meta-historical nature, through contact with a reality that has always been extraneous to it. This is a sort of radical, extreme, realism therefore, capable of shattering the supposed normality of our industrial (and industrialized) culture.

The primitive condition refers instead to the existential reality of contemporary humanity in the savage context of today's metropolis, where fragments of technology coexist with a reality in which dream, memory and myth are closely intertwined. In the Rio Negro Manifesto of 1978, Pierre Restany compared the way we survive in the great cities of the modern world with that of the Indians of Amazonia, who have before them a scenario made up of worship of the dead, magic and shamanic rites, of sounds, colours and smells, of animals and plants; a universe which, like fish in the sea, they never see from the outside but only perceive things as a discontinuous succession of single events, places and experiences; where time is a mythical reality that stands outside history. As Alberto Moravia put it, anyone who lives outside history, lives naked.

According to Pierre Restany this condition is very similar to that of contemporary humanity, immersed in an ocean that lacks a unitary image and whose horizon is never glimpsed. So the contemporary condition is something that does not contradict the logic behind industrial modernity, but bears witness to its extreme and devastating consequences; a totalising form of laissez-faire that brings humanity close to its animal state. A condition that does not mean regression but absolute freedom within a bio-technological environment from which it is not possible to emerge.

If we look at Francis Bacon we see how man, returned to the primordial monkey state, is the prisoner of a zoo set up by an elegant and aseptic modernity from which, as Gilles Deleuze noted, he can only seek to escape down the plughole. This savage reality is all around us; the return to the origins and to primordial freedom finds expression in today's practitioners of parkour, who leap over the barriers and precipices of our suburbs like sacred monkeys.

Like the voguers who live completely immersed in the reality of the media, where reality and reality show coincide, possessed by icons and immaterial myths to which they are able to give physical form; resembling shamans possessed by divine spirits. Like the young metropolitan hermits called hikikomori who live naked, shut up in their micro-environments and linked to the outside world only through technologies of the media.

These extreme existential realities, seemingly devoid, as they are, of a strategy and a common purpose, and fruit of an apparently inexplicable energy, can be discerned in the spread of tattooing and piercing, irreversible marks whose magical or decorative significance testifies to the permanence, within a provisional and highly complex universe, ruled by the laws of chaos, of a visible sign that will accompany their bearers unchanged until their death. Thus the primitive condition of contemporary humanity is a continual overlap between total freedom and desire for eternity; the eternity of the human species and the transitory nature of the material world.

Anthropology, as the science that studies human behaviour, is unable to interpret this interweaving of biology and artificial memory, of instinct and artificial steering, of natural conduct and possession of the artificial. The evolution of humanity is not over, but has entered a new phase; the material environment is tending to become dematerialized into pure mythological imagery; theatre of a vital energy that is uncontainable because it is already internalized. So primitivism is nothing but a new level of our normality.

Code Noir

BY LIDEWIJ EDELKOORT

Since the dawn of time, black has had a lot to tell: it expressed mourning, poverty, denial, revolt and exalted the avant-garde as well as the haute-couture; at once Rive Gauche and Rive Droite. From lacerated and studded leather to the perfection of the little black dress, from brutal bondage clothing to a gorgeous prom gown, and from modest mod turtlenecks to modern monks' hoods, the same colour has seen a lot of ink flow in blacks or almost-blacks. It is able to express love and romanticism as well as hate and racism, in equal proportion and with the same ardour.

Black matter will be forever engraved in our souls: film noir, cafe noir, blouson noir, pinot noir. Now black is lustrous and magnificent, like the tail of a magpie, the feathers of a raven or the shiny coat of a horse. Black can be seen in the lace of a domination mask, in a veil of seduction or as a burka of discretion. However, behind its dark shadow hides a myriad of attitudes, divergent tastes and disparate characters. Black reflects opinions like a sign of the times.

To stay contemporary, black is imposing itself in romantic and even frenetic expression. With a return to rural life, folklore and rituals, comes a deep respect for an everyday spirituality; a better local life. A romantic philosophy that fuels great experiences and escape, and a visceral craving for landscapes to explore other horizons in life. A wish to disappear also, like an urgent desire for anonymity. An abstraction like a retreat, through the study of black, the expression of matter, or a cry for help. Today's romantic icons kill themselves, loose themselves and disappear.

As such, revisited romanticism can be seen as a reaction against reason, capable of enhancing the mysterious and the fantastic. A new form of romanticism to escape from reality and enter into the enchantment of dreams, finding the sublime in the morbid and millions in a skull. Vanities in fashion and design, calling us from beyond the grave.

Henceforth, the grand return of cloaks and redingotes, of long dresses and sweeping skirts. All underscored with boots and crowned with hats and bonnets. Painter's shirts, cigarette pants, monk robes and terrorist hoods. Ironically, fashion will mix various religious elements to create a shared point of devotion. And so, black is sketching out life, silhouette and fate — all at the same time.

In this chaotic century — one which still cannot find its way — it seems that there is only one way out, one direction to take. In some form or another, we are merging opposites and erasing contrasts, to embrace and exploit the hybridisation of the various artistic disciplines. To abolish bipolar thinking in favour of universal reflection. Suddenly, black seems to be a federating force: textile becomes architecture, drawing pretends to be installation, volume is seen as flat, painting becomes embroidery, while the photograph is read as a monochrome and videos sell like paintings. We are witnessing an artistic scene in fusion, in which all the arts combine to make a single movement, a single vision and a single discipline, addressing all the senses, suspended between the two dimensions.

This is probably why black has come back so strongly, because all can be merged into it and anything can unite within it. Blending genres, black becomes silent and dull; it can absorb anything and erase everything. A black hole. A way to move forward, to re-centre and shade-off our differences.

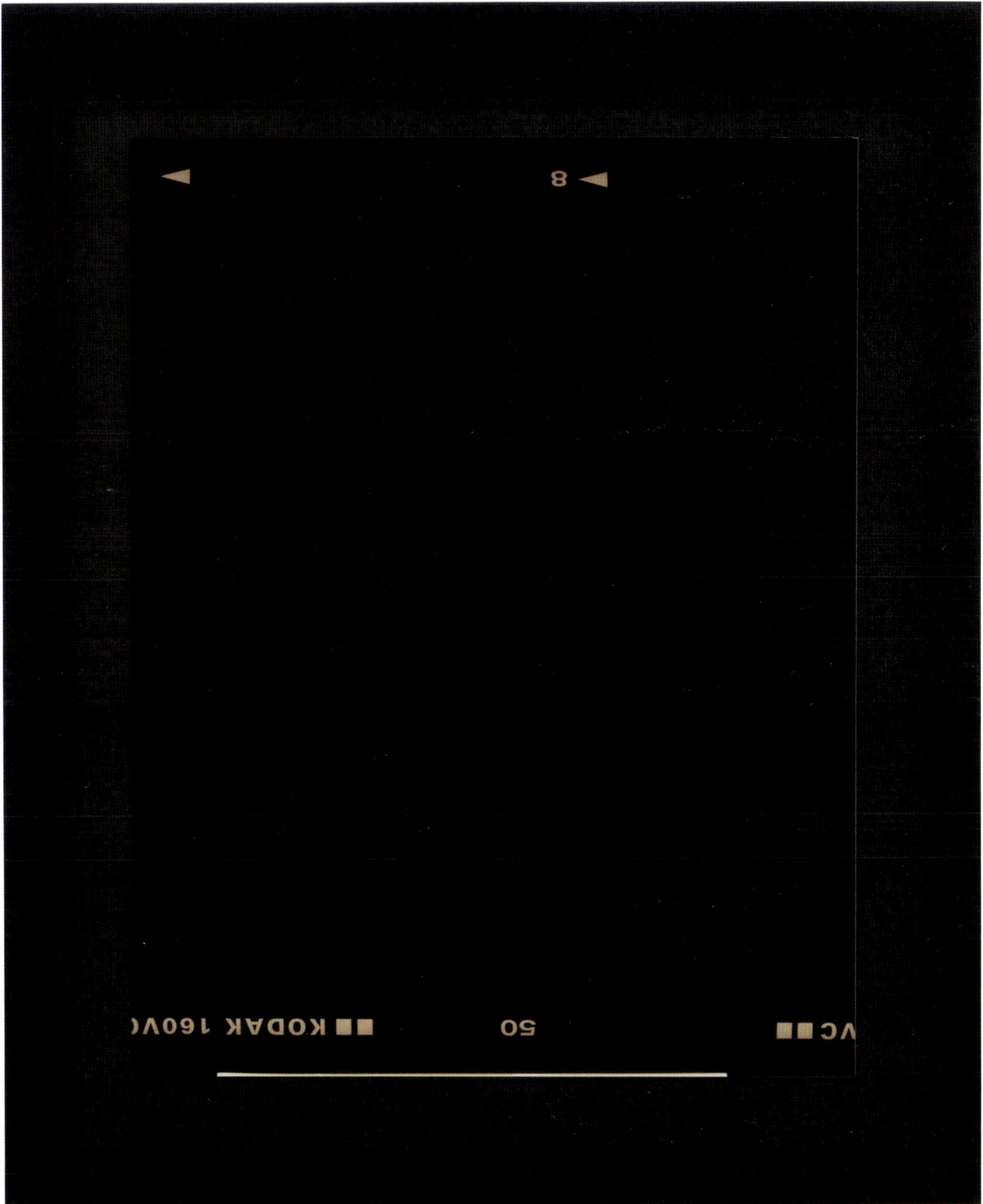

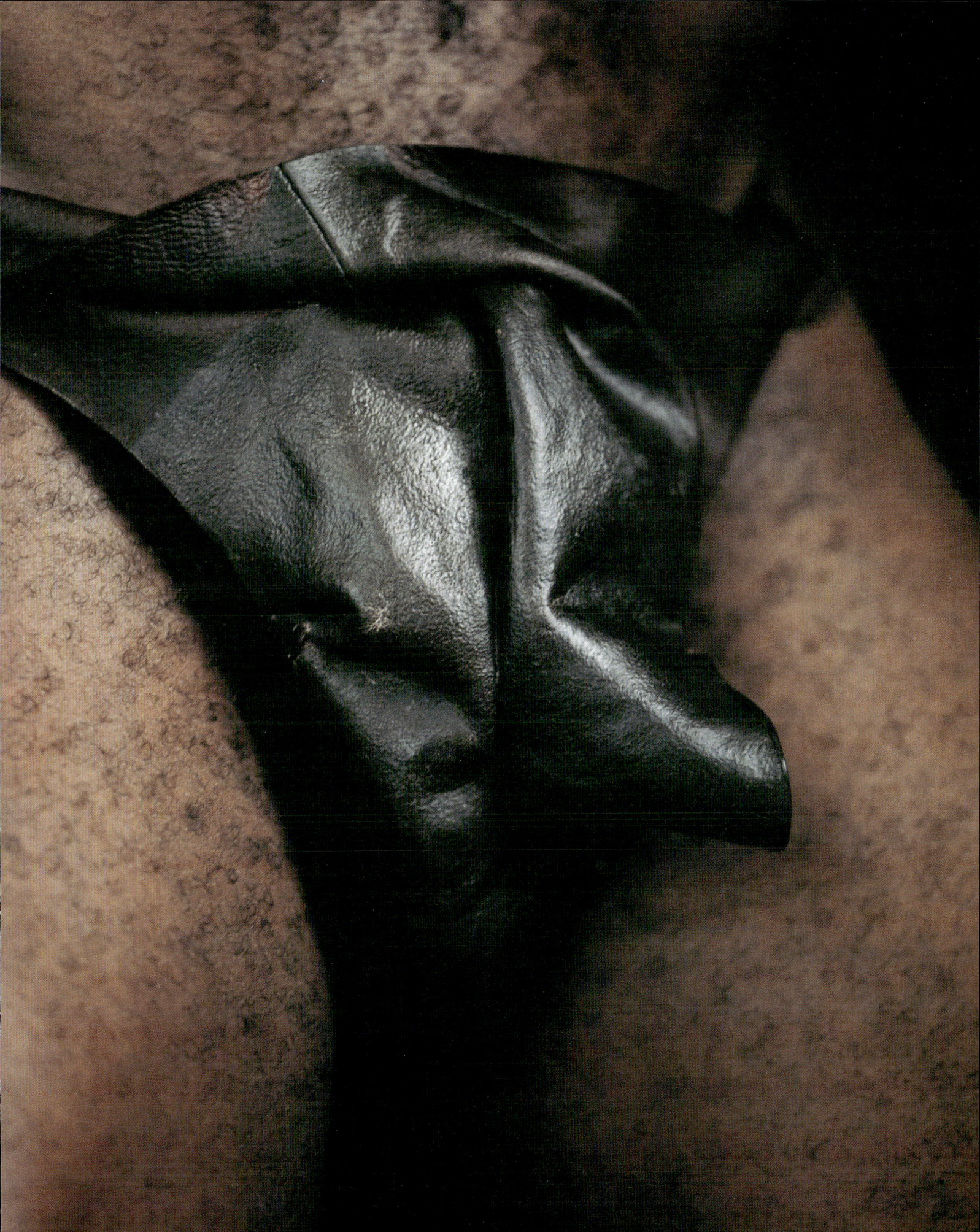

Fetisso Plays Brand Brand Plays *Fetisso*

BY DR DAWID WIENER
PHOTOGRAPHY BY DAVID SARFATI

When the medieval slave traders from West Africa coined the notion "fetish" to describe a kind of magical relation between material objects and human beings, they involuntarily brought to life semantic entity, which, several centuries later, would become brands' *Anima*. At the same time they brought about something of a "sinister pedigree", in the words of the acclaimed fetishism researcher William Pietz.[1] He was one of the first to connect "fetish" with the Portuguese pidgin word "fetisso" and he claimed that it acquired its meaning in the context of colonial trade, bridging two cultures that were practically incomprehensible to each other. Traders used the term "fetish" to describe objects worn or ingested by the Africans, which were thought of "as though" they possessed personal powers that could be transformed into the material world of objects.

What is a fetish then? According to Wyatt MacGaffey the fetish is irreducibly material, which represents an immaterial "something", located elsewhere.[2] It's the fixation of a unique originating event that has brought together previously heterogeneous elements into a novel identity. The fetish, whose power is to repeat its originating act of rearticulating these heterogeneous elements, also fixes desires, beliefs and narrative structures. Early travellers to West Africa were puzzled because gold was valued by the West Africans and yet exchanged by them for articles that the Europeans considered worthless. The material fetish as an object established an intense relation with, and exerted power over, the desires, actions, health, and self-identity of individuals whose personhood was conceived as inseparable from their bodies.

From the very beginning we can find two major problems with the fetish, and both concerned economical dimensions and what easily connects us with the contemporary "branded" world. It's obvious to say that objects possessed so-called "exchange values" however this exchange value easily became "useless" in the context of the fetish object. Africans would overvalue "trinkets" as fetishes when we apply our purely rationalistic approach. Although it could be often highly profitable, trading such items became much more complicated than "rational" exchange would require because the object of desire held personal, social, and/or religious value in addition to its exchange value. In short, what was

regarded as the "secular" rationality of the market broke down in the face of the fetish. This breaking of the exchange value by the fetish is a hallmark of the modern marketplace and one of real power for brands. Furthermore, we frequently have found ourselves required to swear oaths on a fetish object as Africans once did. Instead of entering contracts between autonomous, rational individuals, we have had to enter social and personal experiences via daily "religious" ceremonies of consumption. This also constitutes a modern understanding of brand experience. From this perspective, all brands are somehow of African origin. Objects as fetishes have had to disrupt "rational" and economical exchange trade in order to facilitate the launching of brands.

No wonder that the concept of fetishism attracted Karl Marx, as he expressed his theory of "commodity fetishism": *Through this substitution, the products of labour become commodities, sensuous things which are at the same time supra-sensible or social... I call this the fetishism which attaches itself to the products of labour as soon as they are produced as commodities, and is therefore inseparable from the production of commodities.*[3] And when forty years later Freud empowered fetishism of commodities with the sexual powers and rituals of the sub-consciousness puzzle, a semantic cloud of meanings tied with it started to act in the context of experiencing the consumerization of objects to create brand power as we know it.

Look closer. Experience involves a number of modes of human relations with material objects: a physical relation that has to do with shape, colour, texture, strength, flexibility and possible movements.[4] This is what distinguishes material objects from other cultural objects. The physical properties of material objects lead to a set of limitations on their capacities, thereby articulating the uses by subjects. But objects are used within cultural practices that also specify and constrain their use and they are signs in themselves that locate the object within cultural parameters including time and space. It is through these different modes of interaction that subjects realize the capacities of material objects. Obviously, some objects are experienced more through one mode than another, and the orientation of the subject will affect the mode. It is in the process of consumption, which refers not merely

to the purchase of objects but to the use, enjoyment and disposal of the capacities of those objects, that a relationship between human subjects and material objects is established. The human subject derives the benefit of various "abilities" when he interacts with material objects that enhance his capacity in a number of ways.

The power of objects are not a re-interpretation of the object's material form but emerge in the social milieu in which it is consumed. This fetish quality is attested through ritualistic practices that celebrate or revere the object, a class of objects, and items from a "known" producer or even the brand name of a range of products. These ritualistic practices will involve expressing desire for the object and fantasising about its capacities prior to its consumption. The object itself becomes a sign for these fantasised and desired powers so that its use or enjoyment can re-stimulate the play of fantasy and desire. Unlike sexual fetishism where the fantasy is usually personal, the fetishism of consumption involves social negotiation and sharing the experienced value of the object so the ritualistic practices that fetishize objects will involve action related to the object and its abilities. Expressing desire for and the approval of the object, celebrating it, revering it, setting it apart, displaying it, enthusiastic use of it, are the sorts of practices that fetishize objects. The cumulative effect of these practices amount to an exaggeration of the object in that it is not merely consumed but, in addition, the object can be enjoyed at the level of imagination, fantasy and desire. As a brand.

One way that social and personal value and/or experience is established is through the demonstration of extra powers in the object, which cannot be used in any other way than as a sign of this valued experience and delivery of human qualities: love, power, authority, sexuality, security, status, intellect, and exoticism. Provided that others recognize the extended capacities of the fetish object, they will also recognize these capacities to those associated with it. It is not then the object that indicates its fetish character, but what it means as a sign of social value. Identifying the fetish is not a matter of judging true or real abilities in the object but recognizing the multiple sources of positive experience that is establishing its value. It is the cumulative effect of these multiple sources that approves its power and significance.[5]

Branding and advertising, as well as the evaluations of objects in interpersonal exchanges, have not only created a market for "objects as products" but have also defined modes of consumption of branded content. Use of an object "displays" its powers to others who might then desire to use the same or similar objects. It is through these practices that they become fascinating, acquire a "special status", and become revered or worshipped for how they might evoke new needs, desires and enhance human capacities. The fetishization of consumption is much the same for a work of art as it is for a jacket or shoes. In this context objects are not merely sacrificed by the claims of producers, commentators, curators and critics, they are subject to a negotiation of their powers and of their experiences to users. Desire for objects emerges: to know what one wants, one first has to know what it is and what it might do.[6] They are not mere commodities with extra valuation (social or personal), they become immaterial but real experiences and hidden desires in the more and more de-commoditized world. This desire constitutes what a modern brand could be. And in the cases of the most desired brands, what they really are: object-driven sexual imaginations and fantasies rooted in the experience of the magical rituals of consumption and its derivatives.

In this sophisticated game, fetishized objects become brands. Brands become new fetishes. "Fettiso" plays its own branded game, brand plays by means of "fettiso": the *Anima* of enslaved Africans brought by Portuguese traders is in continual re-birth in our experiential world.

Every day we play this game.

1   Willialm Pietz, The Problem of the Fetish, I, (1985). RES: Anthropology and Aesthetics, 9, 5-17; Willialm Pietz The Problem of the Fetish, II: The Origin of the Fetish. (1987). RES: Anthropolgy and Aesthetics, 13, 23-45.

2   Wyatt MacGaffey, African Objects and the Idea of Fetish, (1994). RES: Anthropology and Aesthetics, 24, 123-131

3   Karol Marx, Capital: Critique of Political Economy (1867), 165

4   Tim Dant, Fetishism and the Social Value of Objects, Sociological Review, (1996), 44 (3), 511

5   ibidem, 512

6   ibidem, 514

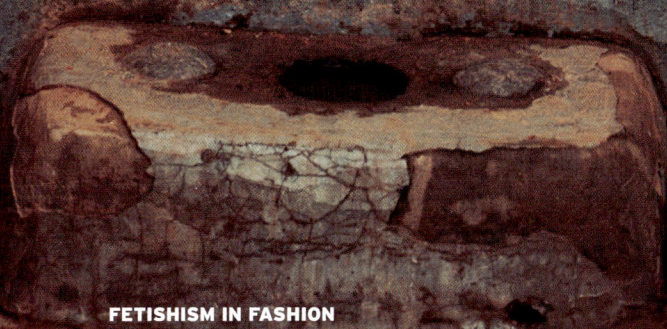

INFANTILE FETISH

Fetishism

BY DR HENDRIKA C. FREUD
PHOTOGRAPHY BY CHRISTIAN TAGLIAVINI

The imagination that dominates fetishism may be able to clarify how an old shoe can be just as exciting as a pretty young girl. What is needed in either case is converting the beloved by way of the inexhaustible powers of phantasy.* We are all familiar with the Grimm fairytale about the princess who is expected to marry a frog. Despite her protests, she has to go along with it. She is rewarded when she shares her bed with him for the first time and he is suddenly transformed into a desirable prince. Sometimes desires are not directed at the whole person but at a so-called part object, such as a breast or penis, or even a shoe, that is to say, a form of fetishism.

Sigmund Freud writes in 1905: *"No other variation of the sexual instinct that borders on the pathological can lay so much claim to our interest as fetishism, such is the peculiarity of the phenomenon to which it gives rise [....] The point of contact with the normal is provided by the psychologically essential overvaluation of the sexual object. [....] A certain degree of fetishism is thus habitually present in normal love...."*

The fetish has far more meaning than Freud attributed to it by focusing especially on the male fear of castration. Just like a stuffed animal or "blankie", a fetish is a "transitional object". It fills the transitional space between mother and infant, the gap when she is absent. It helps in denying the absence of, separation from, and abandonment by, the mother, besides the lack of a penis. The transitional object might be a precursor of a fetish. That which is missing is symbolically represented. With the aid of lacy and ruffled lingerie, the fetish can serve to mask the "terrifying" female genital and magically change it into something beautiful and aesthetic. The beloved becomes a "thing" over which you have power and that won't play unexpected dirty tricks on you. Insisting on having his partner dress up helps the fetishist to cover up an imaginary state of castration, ugliness, dirtiness, or anality, in order to turn it magically into something beautiful, the lady's slip as an idealized lady. When the little boy has grown into adulthood and still denies the difference between the sexes, he is using a mechanism that is characteristic not only of fetishism but of all forms of perversion. A man can get excited when he sees high heels, which undoubtedly serve as a substitute for the missing penis while at the same time, he knows perfectly well the latter isn't there. This idea, which provokes aversion, is banished by actively, even compulsively, looking for the missing body part, this time in the form of high heels. Others will do the same, but as a voyeur in a sauna, by admiring as many penises as possible, whereby the male sex organ itself becomes a fetish.

To sum up: fetishism first and foremost serves denial. Denial of unpleasant or unwelcome facts, like feeling one is born in the wrong body, possessing the wrong gender, but also denial of growing old and feeling ugly. Besides covering up unpleasant or undesired realities it can serve exhibitionism.

This text is an extract from *Men and Mothers: the Lifelong Struggle of Sons and Their Mothers*, Karnac, London, 2012

* Phantasy, as opposed to fantasy is instinct driven.

Aspettando Freud, Gustave © Christian Tagliavini | text © Hendrika C. Freud, Men and Mothers. The lifelong struggle of sons and their mothers, Karnac, London, 2012

Permanent Ink

BY HENK SCHIFFMACHER
PHOTOGRAPHY BY ARI VERSLUIS & ELLIE UYTTENBROEK

MOTHER

"Mother" has always been a popular theme in the world of tattoos, and the first tattoo a young man gets is often associated with this theme, not least because of the ruckus he will avoid when returning home with it. At first most mothers become angry at such an impulsive deed, but once she realizes that this is an indelible display of unconditional love for her and that it will be visible to all for all time, all her heart can do is melt. Nowadays, a truly "modern" mother sometimes accompanies her son to the tattoo parlour and witnesses how the representation of her son's love for her takes shape. Sometimes this doesn't happen, because she has already passed away. A tattoo with the word "Mother", occasionally even coloured with her ashes, can make such a great loss more bearable. The tattoo is part of the mourning process, it provides comfort and nurtures acceptance. The pain is boldly endured, a tear or two might roll down his cheeks, but bargaining about the price is considered bad form.

One of the most beautiful "Mother" tattoos I have seen – probably tattooed in prison on the upper arm of a man – begins the word "Mother", with an M the size of a matchbox, with each letter becoming smaller, resembling the iconic line-up of the Von Trapp family in the film The Sound of Music. The final R was barely a centimetre tall. Was this gradual reduction in letter size the result of an aesthetic choice, or had his love for his mother been conquered by pain?

The word "Mother" is often placed on a scrolling band and is accompanied by such motherly symbols as a heart, a flower, her favourite pet... a combination with a black panther's head or pin-up would doubtlessly be regarded as unfortunate. But the frequently occurring text in the old school English tattoo world – The Sweetest Girl I Ever Kissed Was Another Man's Wife... My Mother – seems to once again be in vogue. It should be stated, however, that the words "Stepmother" or "Mother-in-law" are rarely applied as tattoos. Mi suegra, a Mexican motif portraying a skull with a headscarf and hair curlers, is the only one I know.

TRUE LOVE

"Tattoos last longer than romances" is a common tattoo shop sign. The "True Love" design is, of course, a fool's tattoo. Many a wearer of a romantic tattoo will eventually hear the representative words: "I told you, you shouldn't have done it, you're gonna regret it," and so on.

A tattoo is a sign of adventure and in our Western society there are hardly any good reasons to get one. We don't need to show the hostile native tribe next door who we are. We don't need a painful initiation ritual to step into the adult world. We don't need it in our afterlife or to ward off bad spirits. The only thing we need a tattoo for is to communicate: to tell the world what we think, to give a clear message of love or hate, lust or fear.

True love is for the romantics among us, and testifies to dedication, loyalty and love for someone. Sometimes people are adorned with a romantic tattoo to prove to themselves that these feelings are actually real. Strangely enough they are often seen on the skin of those who are sworn to fun and loyal to none. For them, true love is often a momentary experience, not necessarily a lifelong dedication, meant well and never regretted. Cheers to those who had and have the guts to wear them and celebrate the love of their life, even if there is more than one. Love is a big thing. You can't see it or hold it in your hands but yes, you can wear it on your skin!

GOOD LUCK

Sonny Tufts was a man who definitely burned the candle at both ends. Besides being a highly inspiring and loyal friend, Sonny was a fellow gladiator in the arena of tattooing. An artist known for what we call assemblages – one-of-a-kind pieces, assembled on a bright lacquered background: dices, eight balls, clover leafs, playing cards, horse shoes and lucky numbers.

Wherever Sonny showed up all the lucky paraphernalia would rapidly and mysteriously disappear. Always armed with a screwdriver or a Leatherman, he would cruise the neighbourhoods he visited and unscrew the numbers 7, 11 and 13 from doors, gateposts, whatever... eight-balls disappeared from pool halls, dices and cards from casinos, horses lost their shoes, chickens their wishbones and rabbits their foot. Lucky symbols such as these are used by our industry to assemble good or bad luck tattoos, born to win or lose tattoos, or representations of Lady Luck.

These types of tattoos are frequently worn by people who really need them; people you wouldn't always call winners. Now, I wouldn't call Sonny or any of them a loser, but born to win he was not. He was certainly born to love, though.

ANCHOR

The anchor is the second symbol in the trinity "Faith-Hope-Love", and stands for perseverance and loyalty. In Christian faith it means salvation; the anchor resembling the cross stability is formed on faith.

The anchor stems from the Latin word Ancore and the Greek Agkura, meaning "bending", and is related to the ankle – the Achilles Heel – mankind's weak spot. In the nautical world it symbolizes a completed journey across the Atlantic Ocean. It is by far the most tattooed symbol in the world of seafaring men, also due to its simplicity of form and the respect the object receives as the saviour of the vessel, preventing it from hitting reefs, from going adrift, providing some time to each one's breath, a well deserved break during a difficult trip. In Dutch we say "better to lose an anchor than the whole ship", meaning better to experience a small loss than everlasting sorrow.

In September 2012 I tattooed a tiny anchor on rock legend Lady Gaga. That very same night 200,000 people "liked" this activity on social media: an absolute record. I dedicate this text to her and to another person of fame who we know also had an anchor tattoo: Sir Winston Churchill, especially because he showed himself worthy of wearing this symbol as proves his steadfastness in his resistance to the Nazis. To Winston and Gaga, and may the anchor enjoy an increased interest in the world of tattoos.

Land of Rising Beauty

BY LIDEWIJ EDELKOORT

PHOTOGRAPHY BY ERWIN OLAF

The ability to feel awe and wonder about organic beauty is the essence of Japanese culture. Ever since the aftermath of the natural disasters that ravaged the country in 2011, our eyes and hearts have once again turned to the Land of the Rising Sun, asking their people to stand up and rebuild; inspiring us with their resilience, deep wisdom, sense of style and innovation.

We live in a timeframe where inner-reflection is touching the mind, body and spirit of many — bringing about a Buddhist and Animist perspective. Sharing the ritual of drinking tea, toasting sake, contemplating shadows, and creating ikebana compositions; as well as knowing how to appreciate the recycled and revere the redesigned.

This fetish feeds fashion with an intense thirst for everything Japanese. Taking bonsai and bondage into account, blending fish and flower imagery, and using traditional make-up with new colours, cute and assertive at the same time. Codes of the past are mixed with the behaviours from today to create a brand new kind of fashion which is a hybrid of serenity and perversity; a manga geisha on her night out. Dressed in traditional patterns in futuristic materials, walking on platforms that give her the modest stride of the Maiko, all the while listening to experimental electronic music and covered by a transparent happy coat.

These multiple layers will influence fashion and textiles, as well as in design and interiors. Vintage fabrics will be restored, patch-worked and woven together into new matter. Ikat floral kimono patterns will be blurred and difficult to discern. A devotion to precise detail will entail myriad cute bows and combs, gris-gris and artificial flowers, painted fans and embroidered obis. And the return of the kimono will bring the square back to life, folding garments into sculptural form and wrapping geometry into complexity.

Berger des Landes de Bordeaux.

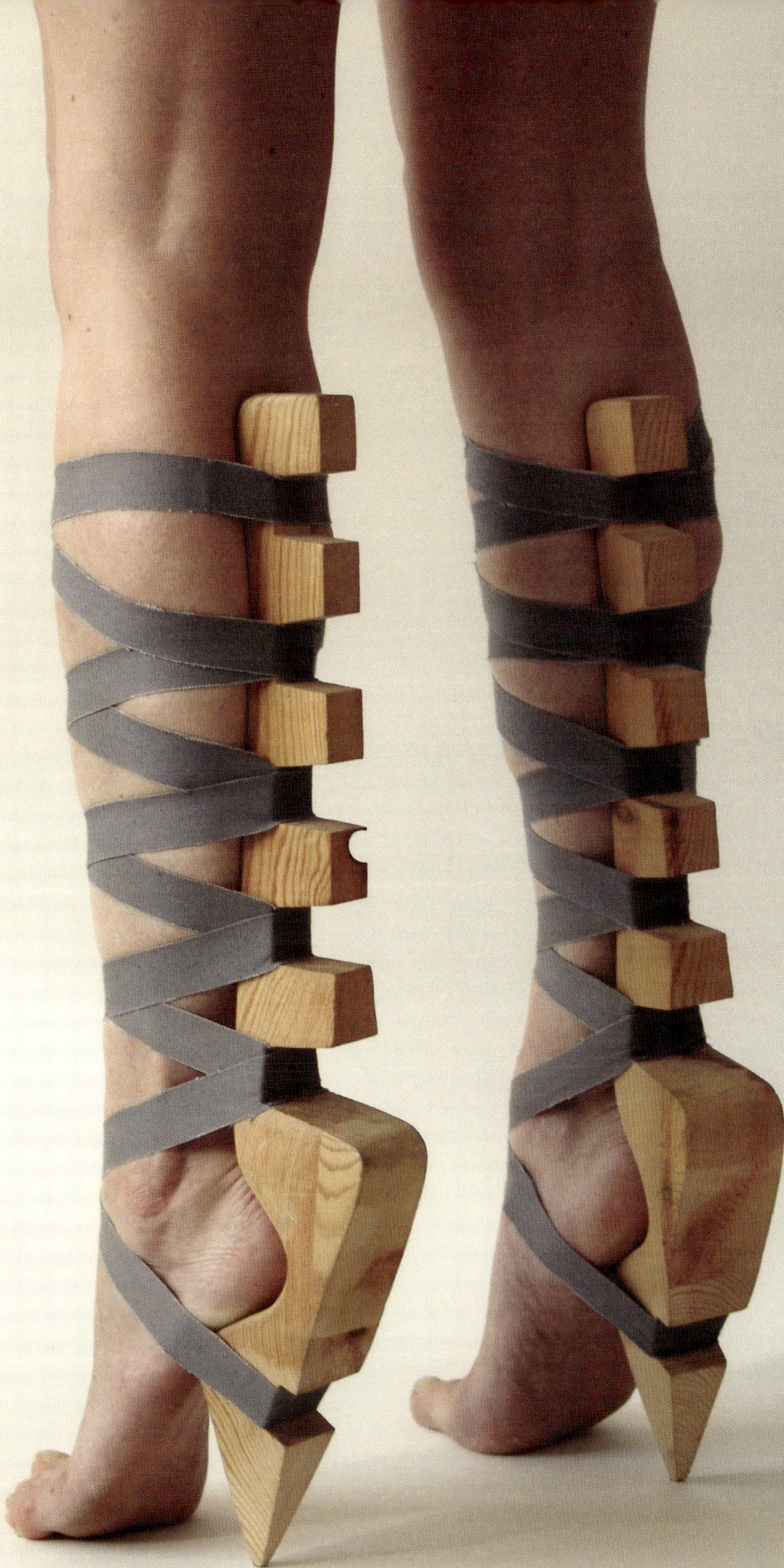

Elevation

BY MARIE JEANNE DE ROOIJ

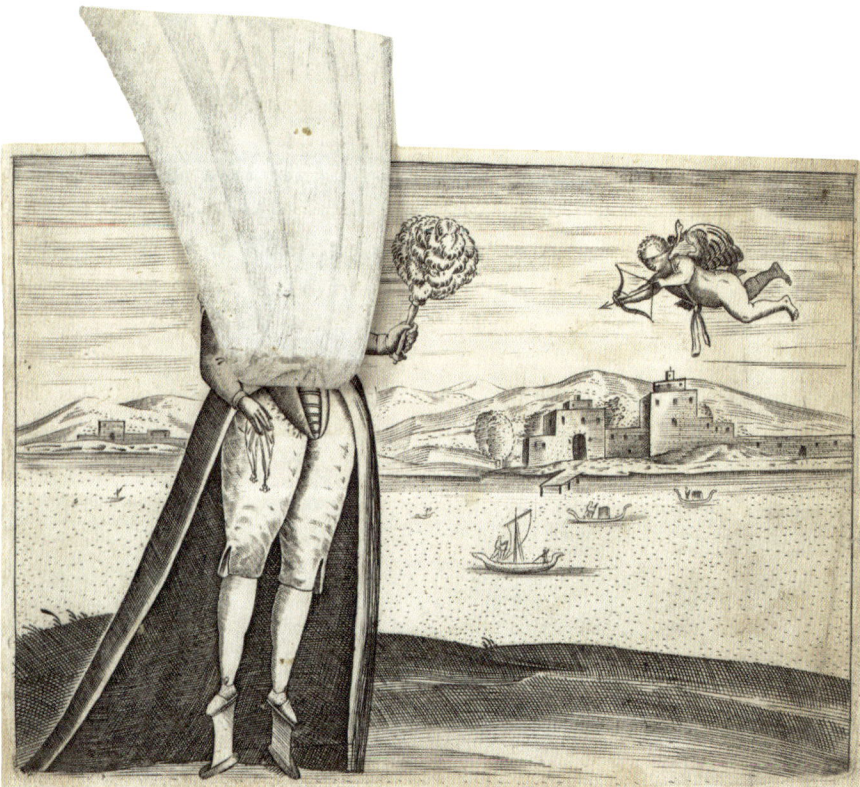

High-heeled shoes mostly worn by women seem to be adored passionately by wearers and onlookers – men and women alike. The craze to have the latest ones, the highest ever, and to wear that special pair no matter what physical impediments are to be overcome, is interesting to contemplate and to wonder why. Where does this on-going craze come from? Have we set foot on similar soil in the past? And how about the fetishistic connotations?

Incredible as it may seem, we have been crazy about insensible shoes more than once; outrageously daring, dangerously eccentric and unpractical constructions even compared to today's over-the-top examples, just think of Lady Gaga's claw-like, shiny unwalkables.

Elevation in contemporary shoe design can be appreciated as a perfect platform to celebrate and cheer on the inventiveness of upcoming new designers who keep pushing the limits of wearability and coming up with new surprising variations on the basics of shoemaking; experimenting with new technologies (such as 3D printing), production techniques, materials and shapes.

Apart from the technical, social, cultural aspects and artistic qualities of shoes, there is always the personal fascination for shoes, especially high-heels, an obsession which goes back a long way, but presents itself differently in each given period. Why do we elevate ourselves, why is height more and more essential for the fashionable shoes we prefer?

In order to survive as a vulnerable species walking upright it is essential to keep your feet safe. Since prehistoric times, shoes have first and foremost been made to make life and walking easier; they protect our two feet against cold and water, cuts and bruises, and they stand between us and the vulnerable immediate contact with Mother Earth. Exchanging clothes is one thing but exchanging shoes mostly occurs only when we have no other option. Way too personal.

As soon as we were "shoed" we started to make distinctions between one pair of shoes and another (not just because no single pair of shoes fits all) but because each pair of shoes becomes a very intimate attribute for the owner alone. People felt the need to set themselves apart from other social groups and classes by being more or less elevated compared to the others. Whether it be walking on stilts or chopines in Venice or wearing elevated clogs in Japan; it was an indication of one's social standing.

Shoes are intimate partners and messengers of what we want to communicate about ourselves to the world around us. And our feet know exactly why it is worth it to take on the challenge of tight high-heeled sisters after practicing perfection at home in front of a mirror.

High-heeled shoes don't just give the wearer a certain social status, they do much more than that to make it up close and personal; high heels make legs look longer and slimmer, feet smaller and wearing them makes us appear taller. That's not all, because high heels work miracles for posture and gait, flexing the calf muscles and making the bust and buttocks stand out more prominently: in short, adding over-all power-dressing sexiness and self-assurance. By the way, this bonus is uplifting for men as well – whether wearing high heels or not.

According to some, the sub-idea that high heels are sexy is because when a woman orgasms, her feet extend; hence, high heels put the woman in a perpetual state of pleasure. Simple as that, and as such it has become a generally accepted notion, but is it true and does it really explain the desire of women to wear and own high heels – and not just one pair, but lots? As always, it is all in the eye of the beholder.

Psychologically- or sexually-infused motives for wearing high heels are easy to find, but the sheer attraction of the shape and beauty of the high heeled shoe can be a pressing incentive as well,

the mere joy of possessing a beautiful or inventive new design. Not just high heels, but also plateau soles and platforms are sought after, often as part of a special subculture.

Maybe people buy new shoes for proven comfort in the same way we treat ourselves to comfort-food. Not healthy per se, it feels more like a guilty pleasure, both soothing and satisfying, which might lead to a (mostly) innocent addiction. In this respect, a certain fetishistic aspect is added to the personal shoe-experience. Wanting to be in the presence of treasured objects that give you a gratifying feeling of well-being has become a normal necessity today. We have come from an era of an economy of need (until the 1960s and '70s) towards an economy of want. Wanting and dreaming are almost twin-thoughts and desires. More and more we project the realization of dreams and fantasies onto desired or personalized objects to fill the unsatisfactory void in our walk-in closet or sometimes even in our lives. A "normal" human condition ever since times when we charmed "spirited" lifeless objects to chase away evil. Today we may not be idolizing sacred or ceremonial objects any longer, but a new pair of shoes from a top designer will do just as well to serve this same old purpose for some of us.

In this time and age, many people are trying in real life to match as perfectly as possible the picture they have in their heads of how they want to look or look like. More and more, they take on the role of a self-made stylist and fashion designer to create their own persona and show their personal fashion-code to the world, often via blogs and social media. And affordable special shoes for every style and personal fashion statement are within reach for many. The pain of tight high heels is then just something you have to endure for the good cause of being the one and only special person you designed yourself to be. And you don't have to wear your uncomfortable signal-shoes 24 hours a day to get your message across.

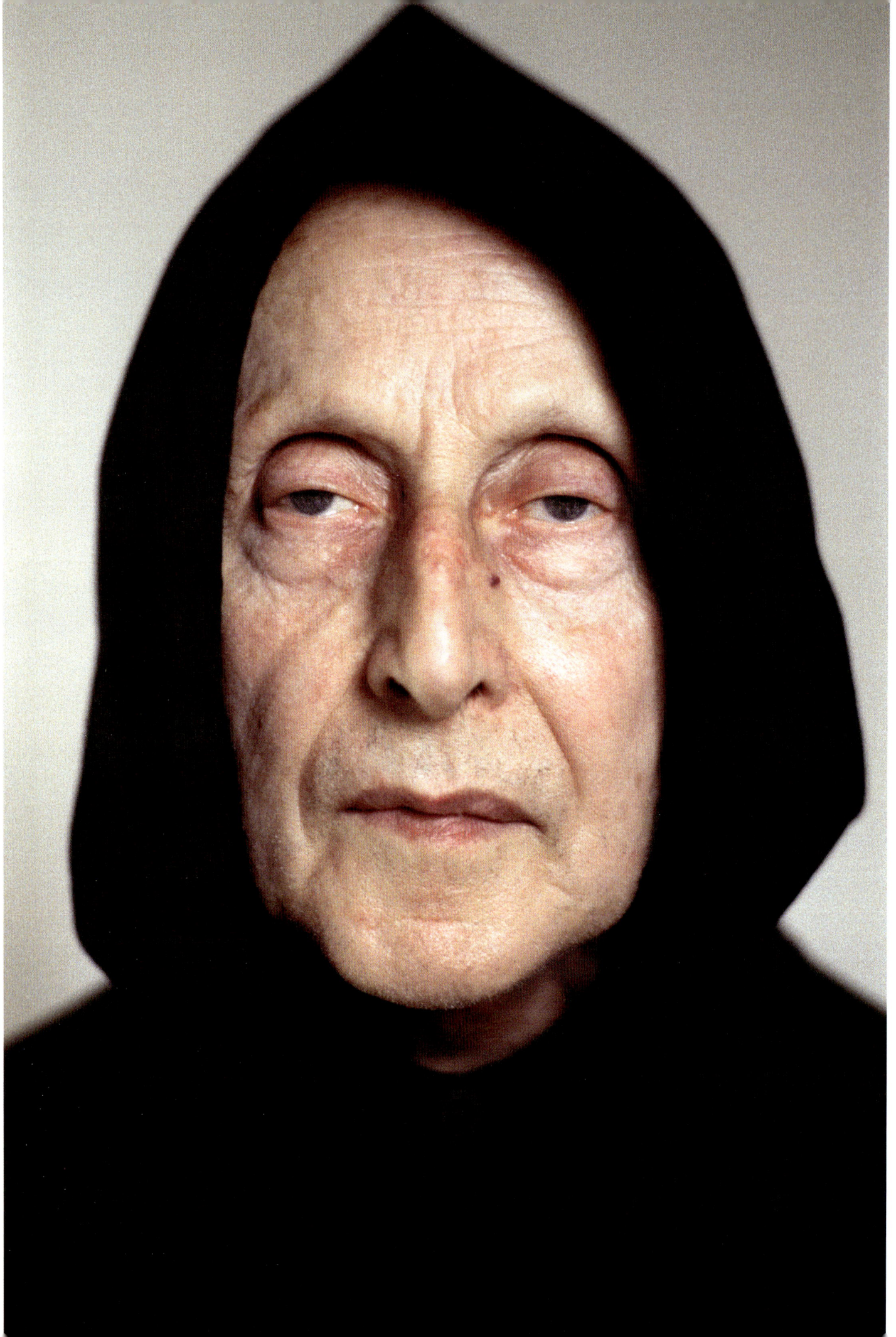

Finding Renewal by Sticking to Tradition

BY DOREEN CARVAJAL
PHOTOGRAPHY BY ROLAND FISCHER

In Cork, Ireland, the Rev. Gerard Dunne has worked for 12 years essentially as a human-resources recruiter — albeit one in a habit cinched with a dangling wooden rosary — for the ancient order of the Dominican friars. Once, his medieval robes may have deterred some. But today he is convinced that the garment is his greatest selling point for enlisting new priests.

Other religious orders largely stopped wearing their traditional garb in recent years, as they tried to attract new followers in secularizing societies. But the friars deliberately went on wearing the robes and promoting the spiritual benefits of shared prayer and a communal lifestyle — with a little help, too, from a chatty blog. "We made a conscious decision a few years ago to wear the habit because we had no vocations and we were in a bad way," said Father Dunne, 46, who estimates that he has travelled nearly a half-million miles along Ireland's country lanes and highways in search of recruits. "If we didn't present ourselves in an authentic manner, who would join us? And that meant going back to the fundamentals."

Those fundamentals — which include the signature white tunic and black capuce of the Dominican friars, fashioned almost 800 years ago — have helped lead to an improbable revival of the Dominican order of preachers. Even as other orders close houses and parish priests in Ireland are vanishing at a time of clerical sexual abuse scandals, the Dominican order is growing, and not just in Ireland.

The friars are something of a hybrid between monks and diocesan priests. They live together in a priory, sharing prayers and meals. But unlike monks, they work in the broader community in preaching and teaching roles in churches, universities and secondary schools. It is a way of life that Pope Francis himself has chosen, shunning the papal palace for a guesthouse to "live in community" with bishops and priests at the Vatican.

In the United States, the largest north-eastern branch is expecting 18 novices to enter its theology school in Washington, which was expanded three years ago. In the smaller southern region based in New Orleans, the Dominicans are scrambling to finance an influx of novices — six this year — with annual expenses of $30,000 for lodging and theology education over seven years. "People see the habit in a much more positive light then clerical clothing, the black shirt, white collar and suit," said Martin Ganeri, who is a Dominican vocations promoter for England, where five people entered the order this year. "The habit doesn't have the negative image of the clergy, the child abuse issue."

In fact the Dominicans have faced child abuse accusations in Ireland. But perhaps because of a garb that harks back to the more austere and disciplined traditions of the church, the Dominican friars have managed to flourish even in the Irish Republic, where surveys show Catholics are deserting the church pews faster than in almost any other country.

In tough economic times, the stability of community may also be appealing, and the resurgence for the Dominicans has coincided with Ireland's economic crisis. But Father Dunne and others said most potential candidates were already prospering in existing jobs in professional fields, and came to the order because of a yearning for greater spirituality.

The revival of the order has been particularly striking in a country where diocesan parish priests have been disappearing. Just 12 men started theology studies for all of Ireland's[26] dioceses last fall — a record low. In contrast, in January a Dominican vocations retreat in Cork was oversubscribed at St. Mary's Priory and two more were added in March and April. The early events drew a total of 20 men to whom the idea of a simple lifestyle and a clear identity appealed at a time of uncertainty in the lives of many.

In the fall, the Dublin-based order enrolled five men, joining 20 other Dominican theology students. They will become part of a community of 175 priests in 18 priories or communal houses across Ireland. Their rising numbers in Ireland have made the Dominicans the envy of other orders, which have sought to copy their recruitment methods. "They're the most successful to the degree that they were online and on the Internet at an early age, and had a blog before the other orders were catching up," said Terence Harrington, a vocations director for the Capuchin order in Ireland, which has taken to Facebook and Twitter. The Irish diocese now has an iPad app for people considering the priesthood.

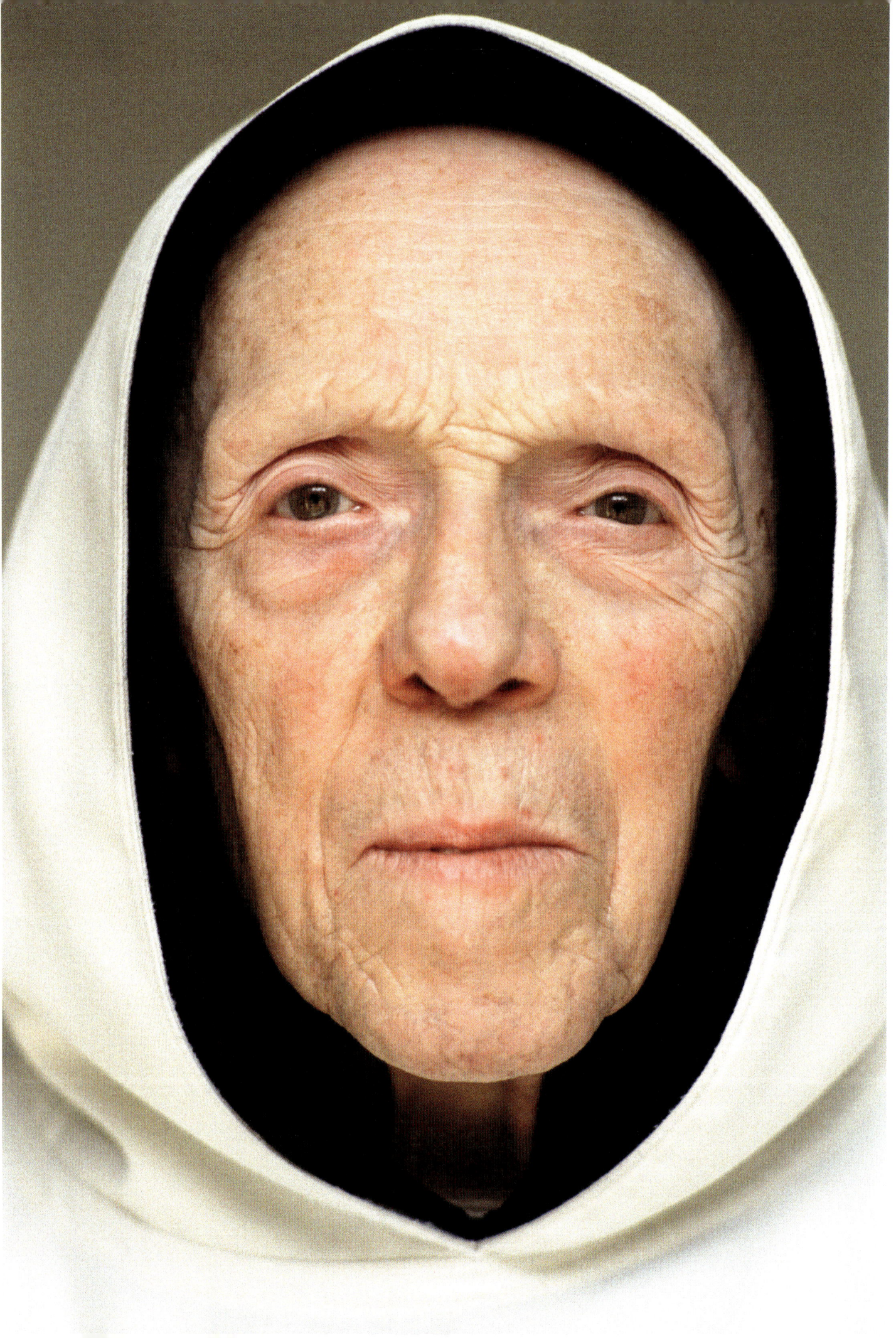

SPIRITUAL FETISH

Typically, it takes eight months to two years for prospective candidates to decide whether to join the order while working with a Dominican mentor, like Father Dunne. With that period to reflect, the attrition rate for new entrants has dropped to 15 per cent, Father Dunne said. Maurice Colgan, 41, a former social worker for drug addicts who was ordained as a Dominican priest in 2011, said he was still adapting to his lifestyle. "My hat goes off to diocesan priests, but I don't know how they do it without community life," he said. "Today, you need the support of your brothers. Now, of course they may annoy you and you annoy them, but that's natural in a community."

At one recent retreat, prospective recruits were invited to imagine themselves as black friars, as the Dominicans are nicknamed, gathering for evening prayer at the 19th-century St. Mary's Church in Cork, where the order first arrived in 1229.

SPIRITUAL FETISH

The guests included a university student, a government lawyer and a school-teacher drawn by the order's Web site, which is stocked with videos, among them one of a friar snowball fight set to the song "Eye of the Tiger." Later, the group crowded at a long wooden table for a traditional Irish fry dinner of potatoes and sausages.

Some of the Irish candidates said they were impressed by the order's rising numbers and openness to newcomers. Matthew Farrell, 38, a former bartender from County Offaly and a novice, said he had sampled other orders, like the Carmelites. "I've been searching a long time for a vocation," he said, "I wanted to get married or wanted to do something else. I tried to visualize myself as a priest." But in the end, he said, the Dominicans won out: "The Dominicans have a lot of enthusiasm and energy, and I liked the fact that they wore habits."

Make Believe

BY MARIE JEANNE DE ROOIJ

When taken out of their original and intended context, religious artefacts, symbols and imagery can be woven into the hybridized melting pot that is global fashion and urban culture today. It no longer seems enough to simply signal subtle hints about who and what you are. The need to create a new self-image and identity in a babelonic age – and to make the world around you believe in this externalised creation of yourself – is apparently and visibly a very urgent one. The ambivalent cultural implications of this ever more visible trend means that people feel comfortable referencing content and meaning from different cultures and religions; not just from Christianity, Hinduism, Islam and Buddhism, but also from Shinto, Sikhism, Jainism, Taoism and more. Inspirations are incorporated into an added message for fashion, street-wear and subculture.

Information is available to everyone. The advantages of the interconnected global village are confronted by our unacknowledged being ending up lost in translation. In order to become a real personality in this world, a person who is wanted and needed, or in fact believed, is forced to build up their self-image and identity from scratch, gathered from the eclectic information we find in the Google-era, via social media and in subcultures; or as examples from celebrities or people we admire – for instance the impact of the crucifix used as a fetish artefact in Madonna's 'Like a Virgin' video cannot be underestimated.

Our body conveys an image of who we are, what we need and where we want to be. But because people are more uprooted than ever before, lacking the stability of common ground for a steady cultural and personal identity, this message has to be communicated more precisely; outspoken to reach the beholder we need, to become recognised as an individual fulfilled person. The whole body can therefore be presented as a fetish; tattoos, colours, symbols, leather, latex, piercings; cryptic concoctions of symbols and signs which signal – read me, unravel me, want me, need me, believe me, I am…

This fetish-in-fashion game of "show and tell" can definitely be studied as an intriguing and arresting cultural phenomenon, especially when the fetish-body is seen as a new and individualised religion to find our identity – personal, cultural, social and political. With these utterly outspoken and visible tokens, tracing back to an eclectic range of religions (sectarian, esoteric, occult, hermetic sources… presumably most of them today found on the Internet), are we able to decrypt secret signs and religious mysticism altogether?

Redefining our self-image and identity in an extroverted manner during these interconnected times, and projecting our personal existence as an object to be reckoned with, are ways of dealing with the challenges of a dynamic, rootless and image-driven society. Within this new context, religious symbols used for this purpose lose their traditional meanings and values, but gain cultural potential in developing new sub-cultures, political awareness and definitions of society's make-over.

Re-mixing to come up with newly energised cultural strongholds is nothing new when it comes to faith; for example, many Christian rituals and festivities were constructed with the relics, symbols and mysticism of former heathen religions. It is the Catholic faith that has the best body-as-fetish example in its inventory, Jesus Christ himself offering his body to anyone who wants to believe in him.

Fashion as the new fetish-religion, we better get used to it.

These endearing portraits of *Nuns and Monks* form part of a series by the prolific German conceptual photographer Roland Fischer. First exhibited at the Musée d'Art Moderne de la Ville de Paris, the images were taken in forty French monasteries between 1984 and 1986. While spending time with his subjects, Fischer discovered that their fetishistic habits were "actually an abstraction of the human body" and therefore their silhouettes could be considered as a photographic equivalent of the "ready made".

Black Fire

TEXT & DESIGN BY SIMONE FARRESIN & ANDREA TRIMARCHI

As part of a commission for the Vitra Design Museum, Studio Formafantasma recently unearthed a fetish for charcoal.

For this project, Formafantasma partnered with Swiss charcoal specialist Doris Wicki, one of the last people dedicated to the tradition of producing charcoal by slow burning wood (5-7 days). The activity, also deeply rooted in Swiss tradition, was economically important when charcoal was produced as a metallurgical fuel, but was banned in the 20th century due to deforestation and CO_2 emissions.

Despite the negative connotations, a few charcoal burners are still operating today. The passing of time has, in fact, morphed this elaborate production process into a nostalgic 'happening', often relegated to festive folk events. In other parts of the world charcoal burning is still a reality. In the Congo, for example, charcoal burning threatens the Virunga National Park, one of the nations biggest natural reserves. Historians have found evidence that carbon filtration was used by the ancient Egyptians, while in Japan it is still common today to use a few, simple charcoal branches to purify tap water.

Formafantasma – whose previous work comments on notions of tradition and nostalgia – draws inspiration from the tension between the dystopian idea of charcoal, causing pollution and destruction, while also being employed in healthcare and water purification. In collaboration with a glass blower and wood carver, Formafantasma produced a series of jars and wooden 'filters'.

Over the course of a few days spent in a forest in the surrounding outskirts of Zurich, wooden pieces were customized; left burning and deteriorating while the process was documented by photographer Luisa Zanzani. The charred remains were further sculpted into a series of elements to be added to in jars. Additionally, a small glass bottle was blown into a hollow carbonized log: the resulting glass becoming opaque and textured where it came into contact with the charcoal, yet maintaining clarity in the rest of the body.

Fashion & Performance: Materiality, Meaning, Media

BY DR JESSICA BUGG

Fashion and Performance

The worlds of fashion and performance have tended to be analysed and understood in the context of their own disciplines as separate and distinctly different, in terms of their design process and intention.[1] However as performance and fashion practice both increasingly move into new and site-specific contexts, and as focus is extended around conceptual and experimental approaches, the divisions between clothing designed as conceptual fashion and clothing designed as costume for performance have arguably become less clear. The subject is timely and two recent exhibitions point towards an extended exploration of the relationship between the two disciplines in respect of both methodology and practice. *Arrrgh! Monsters in Fashion*[2] highlights the growing exploration of character in fashion and *Ballet and Fashion*[3] addresses collaborations between fashion designers and ballet.

In her book *Couture Cultures*[4], Nancy Troy identifies a growing cross over between theatre and fashion in contemporary fashion practice.[5] I use the term *performance*, as opposed to *theatre*, as it offers a broader reading, by encompassing music videos, film, live performance, opera, contemporary dance, street performance, mime, pop up performance, immersive and site-specific work. Troy alludes to the breadth of practices emerging at the intersection of fashion and performance, that includes fashion practitioners designing costume for dance and opera[6], the application of narrative and performative communication in fashion photography, and the increasing endorsement and promotion of fashion by celebrities, film stars and pop stars who wear designer's clothing in performative advertising campaigns and music videos. It is, however, contemporary performance of the clothed body in catwalk presentations that is most clearly associated with performance in a holistic sense, where the mechanics of performance and the stage have been employed.[7] Caroline Evans discusses the development of mannequin parades in the early 1900s and their progression into blockbuster spectaculars, referring particularly to 'the spectacle, excess and showmanship' of Alexander McQueen and John Galliano in the 1990s.[8] She extends this discussion in her seminal text *Fashion at the Edge*[9] where she addresses *experimental fashion design* and increased spectacle within fashion communication. In the case of these designers, despite the performative approach to communication, the garments themselves remain fashion and are not driven by a performance intention, rather this treatment was applied to the collection to assist in the promotion of the designer and the collections.[10]

Beyond this a type of *fashion performance art* has emerged within areas of conceptual fashion design practice that builds on a history of artists working with clothing and the performing body.[11] The work of Hussein Chalayan, Martin Margiela, Rei Kawakubo, Boudicca and Viktor and Rolf resonates in this cross-disciplinary territory, challenging fashion and exploring the potential of cross disciplinary practice and communicating themes, ideas and messages through the clothed and performing body. These designers embrace performance on a deeper level communicating embodied narratives, processes and ideas.

It is often assumed that the difference between clothing designed for performance as opposed to fashion is the focus on character, narrative, spatial and temporal aspects of performance not usually associated with fashion, which is seen to focus on contemporary aesthetics and the market. However the examples of fashion design and communication discussed here have some form of message or visual narrative that drives the rationale for a performative communication; the process and message is the focus as opposed to the consumption of the garment as product. The performative response in these instances allows the designer and their collaborators to communicate through the clothed and performing body, through either narratives or concepts embodied in the garments themselves, or the physical potential of the garment worn in movement.

There are shared areas of process and methodology that go beyond current discussion of character, narrative, spectacle and performance in fashion communication which are manifest in a variety of ways. What is most interesting, however, at this interface is the transferability of areas of the design process itself and the role of clothing in overall communication. Both disciplines work with cloth, the body, embodied meaning, semiotic codes, exploration of time with reference to the past and present and both speak to an audience of some kind in the present. While not all performative applications within fashion are performance or that contemporary aesthetics, themes and use of fashion spaces in performance[12] are fashion but rather that there is a particular and growing area of practice in both disciplines that seems to function close to or at an intersection.

Materiality, Meaning, Media

Currently some of the most performative approaches are evident in fashion films. Some are developed with more performative integrity than others, notably Gareth Pugh's evocative presentation[13] (A/W 2009) filmed by Ruth Hogben which demonstrates a developed use of the medium as a means of communicating a garment's potential and the intention of the collection through the embodied experience of the wearer. Aitor Throup's work with Jez Touzer goes a step further and uses film to convey a physical and emotional narrative that responds to the devastation of Hurricane Katrina in 2005.[14] Boudicca and Hussein Chalayan have both employed time based communication to expose the performance in the design process itself.[15] The work of these artists and collaborations can be seen to function in a space between fashion and performance, acessable from either perspective or indeed understood in its own right as performance.

Increasingly there is a community of contemporary practitioners who seem to work specifically in the hybrid space between performance and fashion.[16] Fashion trained Di Mainstone works directly with the body, designing performance through clothing by writing stories that are translated into wearable forms. Other artists such as Maria Blaisse, Anna-Nicole Ziesche, Margret Wibmer, Lucy Orta and myself work outside of a specific narrative indicating the possibilities of communicating shared clothing and body related concepts in performance. The design duo Lucy and Bart work in a similar way, creating fabricated body forms that explore character, narrative and meaning through clothing the performing body. Their work has been described on their blog as 'instinctual stalking of fashion, architecture, performance and the body'.[17] The Japanese artist Pyuupiru uses clothing, make-up and prosthetics as a means of exploring identity[18], producing clothing, images and short performances that deal with contemporary issues.

The Body as Site

What is notable in both disciplines is the use of the *performing body* as a catalyst and site for creation and communication of meaning. Fashion theory has increasingly embraced the concept of the body itself as a site for communication and more specifically the generation of concepts and communication of meaning.[19] In her book *The Fashioned Body*, Joanne Entwistle importantly identified that although there was writing on discourses of the body, it had not been related to embodiment.[20] She identified fashion as a 'situated bodily practice' that needs to take into account the lived and experienced elements of wearing fashion and dress, going on to say 'Dress in everyday life is about experience of living in and acting on the body'.[21]

This perspective points towards a shared platform from which to understand the type of experimental clothing design practice that is evident in both fashion and performance that can be understood as 'situated bodily practice'. It also suggests that performance does not necessarily require a linear narrative or story, it is the body itself that connects the designer, wearer, and viewer through a shared understanding of wearing clothing and embodied experience.[22]

In her book *The Actor in Costume*, Aoife Monks highlights the significance of these ideas to performance and costume design, specifically identifying the role of costume in the production of meaning between costume, performer and audience[23] saying 'if we take the work of fashion theorists seriously, who point to the ways in which clothing anchors and produces the social body, and embeds that body with a web of social and economic relations, we might need to acknowledge theatre costume's crucial role in the production of the body on stage'.[24]

This shared embodied understanding of clothing and its relationship to the body enables us to take into account how the emotional and physical factors, as well as the body itself, contributes to the making, intention and reading of clothing based work. It is on this level that we can understand the significance of the clothed body as visual and embodied narrative. The body in effect is the site for the creation of, and communication of, meaning whether that is a narrative, a concept, an emotion or

character. I argue that it is the concept highlighted by Entwistle[25] of 'situated bodily practice' that resonates with, and in many cases drives, the hybrid practice that has emerged between fashion and performance. It is the focus on the body, both physical and emotional, and the experience of clothing as part of a complex performative dynamic that contributes to the making, intention and reading of work within contemporary fashion *performance* contexts.

This is an excerpt from an ebook chapter, Bugg J, Emotion and Memory Clothing the Body as performance in Celia Morgan and Filipa Malva ed. Performance 2 "Activating the Inanimate", Inter-Disciplinary press, Oxford, (2013).

1   This is discussed in more depth in the ebook chapter from which this excerpt is adapted. Bugg J, Emotion and Memory Clothing the Body as Performance in Morgan, C and Malva, F ed. eBook Performance 2 "Activating the Inanimate" Inter-Disciplinary press, Oxford, (2013).

2   Arrrgh! Monsters in Fashion, Benaki Museum, Athens Greece, May-July (2011); Gaîté Lyrique, Paris, France, February-April 2013.

3   Leong R, Ballet and Fashion, National Gallery, Victoria, Australia (2013).

4   Troy, N.J. Couture Cultures: A Study of Modern Art and Fashion, USA, (2003)

5   Troy, N.J. (2003): 81.

6   Bugg. J, 'The Clothed Body in Fashion and Performance', Journal of the Museum of Applied Art 7, (2011). Here collaborations between fashion and performance are expanded upon.

7   Fashion Theory: The Journal of Dress Body and Culture devoted a volume to the subject of Fashion and Performance, Vol 5 issue 3, Oxford, (2001).

8   Evans, C, The Enchanted Spectacle, The Journal of Dress Body and Culture, Vol 5 issue 3, Oxford, (2001): 301

9   Evans, C. Fashion at the Edge, USA: Yale University Press, (2003).

10 Bugg, J, Interface: Concept and Context as Strategies for Innovative Fashion Design and Communication: An Analysis from the Perspective of the Conceptual Fashion Design Practitioner, Phd Thesis, University of The Arts London, (2006).

11 Artists and performance artists such as Rebecca Horn, Caroline Broadhead, Leigh Bowery, Lucy Orta, Azra Aksamija, and Yayoi Kusama, Yoko Ono.

12 Seven Sisters Group performed Double Take (2000) in Selfridge's department store and Boxed in the window of John Lewis on Oxford Street, London (2006). Punch Drunk collaborated with Louis Vuitton, creating a site-specific immersive performance for the opening of the flagship store, Bond Street, (2010).

13 http://showstudio.com/collection/gareth_pugh_paris_womenswear_a_w_09

14 Funeral in New Orleans tells 'the story of five musicians and their fight for survival in the wake of the devastation' http://showstudio.project.neworleans.

15 Boudicca's Tornado Dress, animation directed by Ben Bannister and Hussein Chalayan and Marcus Tomlinson, Ventriloguy Animation, (S/S 2001).

16 Anna-Nicole Ziesche, Jessica Bugg, Di Mainstone, Margret Wibmer, Gareth Pugh and Ruth Hogburn, Aitor Thrope and Jez Touzer, Pyuupiru, Boudicca, Maria Blaisse, Heyniek, Ike Theeuwes, Lucy Orta, Henrick Vibskov, Lucy and Bart.

17 lucyandbart.blogspot.com/

18 Bernhard Willhelm, Henrik Vibskov, Alexander McQueen, John Galliano and Walter Van Beirendonck, have all explored character within their collections.

19 Warwick & Cavallaro, Oxford (1998); Entwistle & Wilson, Oxford (2001), Entwistle, Cambridge (2000) and Fraser and Greco, Routledge (2005).

20 Entwistle, The Fashioned Body, in Bugg, 'The Clothed Body', (2000): 73.

21 Entwistle, The Fashioned Body, (2000): 10.

22 In Bugg, 'The Clothed Body': 73. Warwick and Cavallaro quote: 'The "imaginary anatomy" becomes the point of organization of relations, and it provides a means by which the self can be perceived by others; it is now both subject and object: the specula image is the basis of being in the world,' Warwick and Cavallaro, Fashioning the Frame. Oxford: Berg (1998): 24.

23 Monks. A. The Actor in Costume. Palgrave (2010): 8.

24 Monks, n.d. p.l0

25 Entwistle, n.d. (2000).

The Aesthetics of Love

BY PHILIP FIMMANO
PHOTOGRAPHY BY LARA GILIBERTO

Betony Vernon is an intuitive red head. She is also a designer of jewellery, sculpture and interiors, an author, therapist and consultant; a sexual anthropologist linking the worlds of philosophy and psychology with wellness and passion. It's little wonder therefore that this Botticelli beauty felt more at home in her long-adopted Italy than in the Americas where she was born. Like a contemporary Renaissance thinker, her academic explorations blend seamlessly with a sophisticated sense of style, making her an intriguing figure at the forefront of the sensual design movement she has helped invent. Her acclaimed book *The Boudoir Bible* (Rizzoli, 2013) has been referred to as the new *Joy of Sex*, yet Vernon's work with the aesthetics of desire goes further to open up a ground-breaking domain for well-being and experiential pleasure.

Vernon's Paris interior is a tasteful reflection of her personal mantra: one which, like her book, breaks down preconceived notions and barriers in order to sooth, heal and please the mind and the senses. Like in the design of a yacht, each nook and cranny has been conceived with precision, with customized built-in elements, walls and screens that allow intimate areas to maximise their spatial potential. "This is a place full of love and made for love" she says, "where people feel comfortable about being totally open." Vernon has strived for a space that makes both men and women comfortable, regardless of their sexual orientation: an asexual zone buffered from the city by a courtyard garden, blurring the boundaries between outside and in; enveloping guests with a moss-velvet circular curtain and a spray of leaf motifs that blow across the floor's carpet...

This place is known as 'Eden', a transitional area in which to reflect, recharge and receive her guests. A black pony table sits surrounded by modernist furniture: an armchair by Gio Ponti, a Leopard chest of drawers by Fornasetti and a chair designed by Mark Brazier-Jones, who specialises in decorative metalwork. To one side, a screen speaks to us about mystery and secrecy. Vernon is "fascinated by the flexibility of a space and this is why the round curtains draw off the office and studio area; the roundness has an energy", and in fact there are no other straight lines in the building.

Downstairs the curvaceous forms lead to 'Heaven', a room notably dressed in leather tiling that Vernon created to follow the building, in a material with the ability to breathe. "It's about a codified use of leather," she says when referring to the evocative tanned hide spanning the floors and wall, "it's about the way the material is shaped, and what it's intended to do, how it architects and redefines the body that brings its force. It's associated with silhouette. It's very interesting to see how people react when they realise they're standing on leather."

Leather is a tactile texture that is built to hug the body. "It is not a material someone feeling weak might want to slide into; you are definitely wearing another animal's skin, so there is something – however subconscious – that is empowering and it is a symbol of power and self-ownership. It's a skin that is alive, and walking barefoot on it is to die for! The way that it ages takes the signs of moments; it has a memory."

An articulated 1945 surgical table is Vernon's favourite object in the room; she is in love with its mechanics (and its flexibility; divided into four panels, it can be transformed into a chair). The table's stainless steel is mirrored by a panelled steel fireplace that reignites the former presence of fire in the room when it was used as a kitchen by the nuns of the Malnoué Abbey in the mid-17th century. Contrary to this French terminology for the 'poorly-tied', the underground chamber is today rigged for the ropes, as well as slings and trapezes. "I wanted to create a sensation of being in a medical office in the 1940s, in a cosy and luxurious way that encapsulates and disarms people. It's about reconfiguring taboos and going against categorization. This is a design and lifestyle philosophy, it's integrated and a part of who I am. There's also something very interesting about being underground. There, you're nurtured by the earth, protected and bunkered. I see the effects of it."

At the centre of 'Heaven' is The Boudoir Box, an artisan *coffret* filled with beautifully-crafted tools for clients to whip, spank, tickle, probe and massage themselves into pleasure. Precious materials such as silver, gold, pearl and horsehair are shaped into decorative organic forms that are the epitome of the 'sado-chic' aesthetic that Betony Vernon has defined over the past twenty years. She describes how this nomadic 'salon' came to her as a vision, "an object that allowed me to create a market when there were no shops: a mobile object that transformed a space by bringing a soul element into any hotel room or private interior."

Vernon's Sado-Chic collection of jewellery started quietly in 1992, at a time when New York's underground S&M scene had surfaced in the high-end bondage fashions of Jean Paul Gaultier and Gianni Versace, and when Madonna released a Sex book featuring erotically-charged photography by Steven Meisel as part of a shock-campaign for her latest album. It seemed like a sexual awakening, "and then that was it", says Vernon. Perhaps we were distracted by the Los Angeles riots, the suicide death of a grunge pop star, a Presidential affair with an intern, or the emergence of high-heeled female archetypes in pseudo-feminist sitcoms. Perhaps it was the proliferation of the AIDS pandemic or the other impending fears perpetuated in society; from the fear of ecology to fear of economy, the discovery of a digital galaxy called the Internet and a fast-approaching Y2K. The 1990s were a decade of regression framed by insecurity and Vernon understood that it was too early for a sexualised style revolution to take place.

September 11 provided a wake-up call. "Suddenly, my responsibility as a human and as a designer – as someone who is producing things – was to make things better." The years that followed 2001 saw the dawn of an era of sexual expression; cushioned by an explosion of masks, lingerie and burlesque-inspired boudoir fashions, and set against a progressive acceptance that a healthy sex life could be considered an integral part of our well-being. The world was in the midst of major societal change, and Vernon was able to intuitively and creatively channel its most intimate identity.

Vernon describes fear as our worst enemy. "Societies in which people have not had some kind of exposure to Eastern thought tend to be most fearful. There's so much potential behind it and as Westerners, we are not encouraged. Shedding fear is of crucial importance to all of our progress. As a people, as a community, we *do* create an energy; and the energy that we are feeling in this moment is one of a major shift. It is connected to our overall sense of well-being because if we are all enjoying a healthy sex life – if we are all balanced, eating right and moving our bodies – we're aligned."

Sexual energy has been a primal instinct for millennia, yet in no other decade has our sexuality been so questioned as it is now, and Vernon sees this as a good thing. "Perhaps the next generation will be ready to actually deal with their sexuality on a really open and understanding level." The idea of training sexual skills evokes a whole new educational philosophy to be developed, and her work encourages people to tap into what their bodies can

provide in terms of pleasure. However, the Internet and technology have left what she calls 'pornovores' – those that obsessively watch too much porn – really unsatisfied with their own sex lives and numb to reality. In their attempts to replicate porn fantasy, Vernon perceives that we live in a time of primal masturbation and isolation: "In this moment, between the turning of the century to today, humans are either not reaching out enough or they are hooking up with someone they don't know around the corner, and the satisfaction derived is a little bit sterile; full of fear, and very ego-centrical."

The phenomenon of people plugging into networks such as Grindr or Blendr is somewhat discerning. "Even the sheer name is about 'grinding', and though it's fine to grind, it's often with someone you will never see again or care about. That is spiritually very dangerous because of the fact that I believe our sexual energy is one of the most potent. When we truly make love, something mystical happens. It's transforming and does take you some place else. That kind of experience cannot be tapped into with someone you're just grinding for 20 minutes... and women hunt just as much as men do."

Technology has also meant that there is a lot of sex going on that doesn't use any contact at all, through Skype, webcam or other means, including text messaging apps such as What's Up. Contrary to this current, Vernon's book is a catalyst for opening up our sexual horizons, and comes in the hopes that by sexually empowering the reader, there may be a general change. She is currently exploring the importance of touch in new areas, such as using hugging to help recovering cancer patients, since something as simple as a hug raises Oxytocin levels, even when hugged by a stranger.

Vernon is at the cusp of a moment when emotional and physical interaction has the power to heal. "One of the most grave things that Christianity did was separate the mind and the spirit", yet we are entering a period in which the body and spirit can be recombined, when sexual rituals and instinctive rites can unite for the first time in an aesthetic and design-conscious manner. "There is not any moment when we are more connected to another person than when our peripersonal spaces are shared. There are not many experiences we can have as humans like when we make love to one another. It's the ultimate sharing of space and pleasure." We can't explain it, but no one can take the mystery out of love or sex.

Natura Morta

INTERVIEW WITH FAYE TOOGOOD BY DAVID CLARK
PHOTOGRAPHY BY MARIUS HANSEN

Faye, I've been going to Milan for about 15 years and your Natura Morta midnight dinners from 2 years ago still provide me with some of my most memorable moments and mental images. Images like being fed blackened, tea-soaked eggs by a latex gloved hand, and bread soaked in squid ink, skewered with silver knives, dipped in water and dark sugar as a dessert, and the gorgeous, smoky resin edition of your Element Table. That night transported me to a gothic, erotic and fetishistic place. I think that needs deconstructing... Let's start with the food... Black food. You devised the menu with Arabeschi di Latte, an Italian food cooperative. What did the black food signify for you?

There is something not only seductive but also unnerving about black food. Working with Arabeschi on this project I wanted to create an atmosphere to the midnight dinners that would enhance the concept for the interiors I had created. The black food, whether it was the black eggs or the charcoaled artichokes, was rich in texture and mysterious in form. Making the whole space elemental and primal.

There are other black foods like southern fried catfish, or blacked beans from an entirely different culture, or black olives, and caviar or squid ink pasta from a more refined culture. But this menu was very basic. Why?

It was important that the food was not sophisticated food. I wanted the food to be experiential not gastronomic, to act as another sensorial layer to the interior. It was not about presenting fine delicacies but experiencing something uncanny and surreal in an instinctive way, so in one room we served stale bread dyed with squid ink. Rough lumps of the coal-like bread were served spiked onto old knives. Guests were then invited to dip the bread into water and then sugar. This recipe is in fact a peasant Tuscan dessert but served black it took on an entirely different sentiment.

Do you remember the first black thing you ate?

Soil. As a child I grew up in a small village in England and spent much of my time outside and so the odd inquisitive fist full of soil was digested. Recently I had a baby and many people told me that women often have the urge to eat soil and coal whilst they are pregnant – due to the lack of certain vitamins and nutrients. Rather disappointingly for me, I did not get that urge!

Is black the colour of style?

Yes. Black on black is for some reason a signifier of style. Black is so powerful as a colour, and in its positive form is a signifier for minimalism, confidence and eroticism, but also restraint, aggression, death and decay.

Do shadows interest you as much as light?

Shadows are frightening to me but at the same time they are beautiful. They are the negative spaces around the positive – light. Shadows are more tangible than light – you can see them.

Why dinners at midnight? What sort of atmosphere were you trying to create?

I am afraid of the dark and there is something magical about this time of day. Midnight is a time when most of the world has gone to bed. There is almost something childlike about staying up past midnight. At this time of day our senses are so alert and heightened, allowing our imagination to take over. I also liked the thought of doing something out of hours, something that was not on the 'go to' list of parties during the Milan furniture fair. I wanted people to attend the dinners and leave with a feeling that they had experienced something secret, underground and mysterious.

Does food inform your design? What about sex? Or are they all just sensually intertwined?

Food does inform design certainly. The food designers we work with – Arabeschi di Latte – are in fact trained architects. They decided to create and build with food after becoming frustrated with the constraints and limitations of architecture. Sex certainly informs design. I think this is very obvious in fashion – one is very conscious when it comes to what you wear and the sexual connotations this can give off – but the connections are perhaps not so obvious in objects and spaces. With the materials I used in Natura Morta I was aware of the impact using a latex sling to present the eggs, making people use their hands to eat, covering my chairs tightly in leather, and displaying erotic drawings by Fornasetti, would all have on my guests. The fine line between sex, eroticism, hedonism and death and decay was something I wanted to explore and black was the perfect vehicle for this. Natura Morta was all about trying to understand the dark side of nature and human nature.

OK, let's talk about the latex swing – such a powerful image for me. The main course, of sorts, after the goat's cheese on charcoal chunks, and the brasier barbecued artichoke hearts, was an egg that had been soaked and darkened in tea. In that room, a pile of eggs were cradled in a latex hammock that was suspended across the wall. There was something primal about it, fundamental – a delicately suspended pile of eggs in a strong stretchy material. A beautiful Eurasian girl with an insect-like visor and a long black latex glove peeled the egg and fed it to me. That was an erotic moment. Were you wanting to turn your guests on?
Yes. I was aware that, like with every fetish, some people would be turned on and others would be repulsed. There is a fine line between the two. I think with the element of service and ceremony, the handing over of the egg on a latex-gloved hand created many sexual connotations.

Latex is often associated with fetishism (and also Batman and Catwoman). Is that why you used it?
I used it because I wanted the eggs to appear almost like a sack of insect eggs hanging in the room. Latex, although mainly associated with fetish-wear, is actually a really beautiful textile in its own right.

What do you like about it?
Its semi-transparent quality allowed me to reveal the globular, bulging shapes of the eggs, creating a very abstract form as a result.

In the final room – the bread room – there were editions of your Spade c s that had been covered with thick leather, hand-stitched by fetish leather-wear makers, like S&M leather makers. I wonder what they provided you with that a standard leather upholsterer couldn't?
I think you may be right – the result may have been similar but the process wasn't. Talking to the S&M leather makers and understanding how they work, the way they use the leather and the techniques, gave the pieces provenance and meaning.

Why did you decide to cover your existing design in leather (rather than create a new one)?
The chair was originally launched in a blonde wood. I was quickly stamped with a label of worthiness and put into the British wood designers category. I did not have a problem with that particularly but I really wanted to re-materialise the rural object and show that through changing its material and skin, I could give the innocent wooden chair a new personality and meaning. In leather it is masculine and strong.

In this book, Li Edelkoort is exploring the notion of binding – that we are born with the cutting of the chord, and that we long for binding throughout life. Do you think we seek comfort in constraint? Or freedom from chains?
There is definitely comfort in constraint for me.

Do you think the world is becoming more fetishistic? If so, why?
Yes I do. I am not entirely sure why, but I think its mainly because there is power in a object. With the world becoming more and more obsessed with technology and the digital image, we are becoming increasingly disconnected emotionally and physically from material objects. I think there may be a predilection towards fetishizing an object because of the feeling of separation that the Internet has brought with it. We are all connected, but virtually, not physically.

Can you pinpoint a moment in your childhood where design crystallised as a thing of importance for you?
When I made a swing chair for my Sindy doll out of a shoebox – after my mother refused to buy me one.

Photographic Palimpsest

PHOTOGRAPHY BY SCHILTE & PORTIELJE

Rotterdam-based artistic duo, Huub Schilte & Jacqueline Portielje explore the rich possibilities the digital age offers photography as an artistic medium. The computer has indeed become their experimental dark room.

From the countless images that Schilte & Portielje have amassed in their archives, the pair sample fragments to recompose new forms; creating unfamiliar intriguing beings that evade any chance definition. These black and white subjects hark back to another time, hovering between reality and a different dimension; contemporary visions of Surrealism.

Associating their work with painting, Schilte & Portielje layer their images in veils. Independently generating options over a length of time, their photographs are constantly being digitally transformed, debated and swapped, before the two merge their ideas into one final, sensually-charged being. A new silhouette emerges, one of elegant poise and that is shrouded in mystery.

The Heart in the Darkness

BY SUSANNAH HANDLEY

PHOTOGRAPHY BY SØLVE SUNDSBØ

Alexander McQueen once said that his heart was in his work. More of an artist than a fashion designer, his collections revealed his to be the heart of a desperate romantic, with a darkly compelling desire for sinister story-telling. The themes of our most beautiful dreams and fearful nightmares, he tailored into collections that would simultaneously shock and fascinate the cocktail world of high fashion. Doomed by his own passions, his imagination stalked the grim worlds of Edgar Allan Poe and Jack the Ripper; the cruelties of Highland history and the tragedies of heartbroken poets. He was the Prince of Paradox weaving conflicting sensations into the same metaphorical cloth. His couture pieces tell of ecstasies with a painful seasoning of agony, or the compulsive attraction of the grotesque. For him, the morbid and freakish held the same emotional value as any artwork. He had a fetishistic fascination for the inevitable fate of all natural things, for vulnerability, death and decay. He used scissors as forensic scalpels to strip away the flesh and expose the skeletal structures of the human spine. Made almost animalistic in their forms, these spiny sculptures are like the memento mori of a vanitas painting, it's the way of all flesh to be consumed. Remains are his raw material, of birds, molluscs, of any creature in a deathly battle with the twined demons of our time – greed and technology.

Lust & Spirit

BY LIDEWIJ EDELKOORT

It is the ghost of animism that will change contemporary culture. No longer just a thing of the past, animism will become an opening to the future. A belief system that enables us to find the presence of spirit in a process, feel aura in an object, and sense soul in design. An energy to adore and with which to embrace multiple sources of inspiration, to layer hybrids and herald mobility in a world that will therefore become more nomadic. A world where power is shared and trust becomes an ingredient of progress. Today, the monolithic modernist doctrine is surrendering to a society of choice and connectivity through almost biological function and scientific systems. The experience is the message, and the road ahead offers the promise of transformation.

It is time to liberate ourselves from the shackles of Capitalist Sorcery, like Isabelle Stengers theorised, in order to experience the flexible system of an exploding economy. We will enter a period of Modern Primitivism, as forecast by Fakir Musafar. With the juxtaposition of high technology and low tribalism, the world will invent a pre-modern alternative for industrialisation and capitalism. Musafar speaks of the idea of learning through pain and body play, something modernity has forgotten. Through corporeal modification, piercing and elevation, he connects to practices that can be found all over the planet. It is a ritual to go into trance and encompass the spirit through the absorption of pain. This is where the contradiction of past and future will merge into one circular movement of both elements.

In a touching homage to Marcel Broodthaers, Alexander McQueen created a fitting vision of our hybrid future in the mollusc-encrusted corset on the facing page; a future where fetishism will bond the erotic with the primitive, espousing the animistic and the sexual all at the same time. McQueen encapsulated this movement, from adorning dresses with feathers to braiding wild furs with lace. The marriage of lust and spirit.

ACKNOWLEDGEMENTS

We would like to thank all of the authors, artists, photographers, academics, designers, galleries and agents that have contributed to this special book. Without all your fetishes, we would not have any metaphors with which to illustrate our story.

We would like to thank FRAME Publishers for leaping into fashion with us and giving us the freedom to create the book we had envisioned; a rhythmic roster of ideas and imagery that is vast and rich. Sincere thanks to Robert Thiemann, Rudolf van Wezel and their team and distributors.

The images have been framed for FRAME by ABC: the Amsterdam-based graphic collective that is Anthon Beeke, Jeroen Jas, Mariola López Mariño and Sacha Happée. They have realised an elegant design that will definitely stand the test of time.

The book's flat-plan has had the pleasure of travelling with us through India, Morocco and Brazil, as well as other places closer to home. We would like to thank the entire Trend Union and Studio Edelkoort teams in Paris, Tokyo and New York, for always providing a safety net each time we needed them, especially Vanessa Batut, Sophie Carlier, Wencke Nilsson, Lena Thamm and Silvia Tolaro. In particular, Willem Schenk became the third member of our fetish trinity, and without him, our project would have not been a success.

Fetishism in Fashion would not have come to the fore had it not been for M°BA's invitation to create a biennale of exceptional expression. Thank you to Olga Godschalk, the board members, our six co-curators and the entire team in Arnhem for giving us this unique opportunity.

Several individuals have provided particular support, including Andrea Branzi, Jessica Bugg, Doreen Carvajal, Sylvia Chivaratanond, David Clark, Dominique Fallecker, Malu Halasa, San Ming, Karen Nicol, Erwin Olaf, Diane Pernet, Susanne Piët, Mia Pizzi, RAVAGE, Jeff Rian, Marie Jeanne de Rooij, Henk Schiffmacher, John Sillevis, Cokkie Snoei, Betony Vernon and Dawid Wiener. Marie Taillefer and Sergio Machado have produced the 13 fetishes that open our chapters and other iconic imagery. And Susannah Handley provided much more than a comma for the texts.

Thanks also to Art + Commerce, Chronicle Books, Groninger Museum, KIT Publishers, Museum für Völkerkunde, Oxford University Press, Scala and The New York Times for kindly opening their archives under very tight deadlines.

Valerie Steele set a very high benchmark with her *FETISH: Fashion, Sex & Power* book first published in 1996 and we are in admiration of her for continual fashion inspiration.

This book is dedicated to the memory of Elly Lamaker, who taught Lidewij her first rules in fashion discipline, and whose unique style gave her the guts to know when to break them. Her legacy has formed and informed generations of students ever since.

And thank you to all the others we have encountered along this journey into fetishism,

Lidewij & Philip

COLOPHON

FETISHISM IN FASHION
BY LIDEWIJ EDELKOORT
EDITED BY PHILIP FIMMANO

This publication accompanies the following exhibitions:

TRAPHOLT

FETISHISM, TRAPHOLT Museum, Denmark
March 12 - November 15, 2015
www.trapholt.dk

MºBA

FETISHISM IN FASHION, MºBA, Arnhem, the Netherlands
June 9 - July 21, 2013
www.fetishisminfashion.com • www.moba.nu

cover:
photography by Marie Taillefer • art direction by Sergio Machado

graphic design:
Jeroen Jas, Anthon Beeke Collectief b.v., Amsterdam

printed by:
IPP Printers, Breda, the Netherlands

published by:
Frame Publishers
Laan der Hesperiden 68
1076 DX Amsterdam
the Netherlands
www.frameweb.com
distribution@frameweb.com

Trade distribution United States and Canada
Consortium Book Sales & Distribution, LLC.
34 Thirteenth Avenue NE, Suite 101
Minneapolis, MN 55413-1007
T +1 612 746 2600
T +1 800 283 3572 (orders)
F +1 612 746 2606

Trade distribution Benelux
Frame Publishers
Laan der Hesperiden 68
1076 DX Amsterdam
the Netherlands
distribution@frameweb.com
frameweb.com

Trade distribution rest of world
Thames & Hudson Ltd
181A High Holborn
London WC1V 7QX
United Kingdom
T +44 20 7845 5000
F +44 20 7845 5050

FRAMƎ

ISBN: 978-94-91727-13-9
© 2013 Frame Publishers, Amsterdam
2nd printing, 2014

Printed in the European Union
98765432